BE YOUR OWN

Inspiration

BE YOUR OWN

Inspiration

BY DR. CHRISTINA RAHM

PART OF THE CURE THE CAUSES STORY

gatekeeper press™
Tampa, Florida

Be Your Own Inspiration: Part of the Cure the Causes Story

Published by Gatekeeper Press
7853 Gunn Hwy, Suite 209
Tampa, FL 33626
www.GatekeeperPress.com

The cover design, interior formatting, typesetting, and editorial work for this book are entirely the product of the author. Gatekeeper Press did not participate in and is not responsible for any aspect of these elements.

Library of Congress Control Number: 2022951902

ISBN (hardcover): 9781662934285
ISBN (paperback): 9781662934292
eISBN: 9781662934308

Dedication

This book is dedicated to my parents, my children, and "The TRINITY." I love you all and am inspired daily by your lives.

Table of Contents

Acknowledgments

I want to acknowledge my children, my parents, my sister, my brother, and my significant other, Clayton Thomas, for giving me the time and space to write this book. I also would like to acknowledge the support I have had for this book from the Ambassadors and consultants at "The Root Brands," "Dr Christina Rahm," "International Science Nutrition Society," "Cure the Causes, INC.," "Under the Red Chandelier, "Bill & Coo," "Ella Pure," "Rahm Roast, "and "ENVIREM." The hard work of the companies and their people have been imperative as it pertains to editing, graphic design, photography, formatting, and directional oversite on the book. Joy, Jayla, Joni, Tyger, Abby, Joni, Duquesne, Preston, Dylan, John, Leslie, Tiffany, Stephanie, Ted, Clayton, Lisa, Brad, Kline, Steve, Karen, Andy, Nick, Ahmet, Matt, Patrick, Nicole, and Mary Margaret—thank you! AND special thank you to the TRINITY!

I spent my life reading and learning about heroes that served people while they also led people. I have always been inspired by people in history that do both in such synergetic ways. BUT true inspiration doesn't come from a book, it comes from people in our lives. My teachers in school, my friends I have had, my uncles and aunts, my sisters and brothers are all people that have inspired me—they need to be acknowledged. AND I always say that my grandparents and parents were my main inspiration, until I had my children. When I had my children and I held each of them, they inspired me in different ways just when I looked into their eyes. Now that they have grown, they inspire me even more. I cherish this! I acknowledge daily that they are the best part of me, and I want to acknowledge that for this book. I also want to acknowledge the unconditional patience and support that Clayton Thomas has given me. I am so thankful for him! Finally, God is my daily inspiration for life. He is why I do what I do. Without God, I am nothing. He will always have my utmost love and respect. Anyone that knows me knows that I only answer to Him, and He inspires me daily to love bigger and better.

Introduction

Life is a beautiful puzzle. We are each imperfect pieces to this puzzle. Since we share our DNA with everything, even with a leaf of grass, we should understand that we interact in different ways with almost everything. I love the fact that we are connected in life with everything, from a mouse to the root of a plant. We each matter, but so does the leaf, the root, and the plant. We are intertwined in one another's existence, even though we may not understand every aspect of this.

I find peace and solace in this. I enjoy sharing aspects of every fabric of my being with even the smallest things in our world. This and so many other things inspire me. Every day I wake up, I spend at least an hour thanking God for these small things and for the bigger ones. I take the time to remember the people I met the day before and the things I dream about or see throughout the day and the night. I remember my dreams, and I pray for guidance on how to receive and use these messages from the world and my subconscious. I focus on the past, the present, and the future. I give thanks to my family and friends, and yes, even my enemies. I ask for directions on the lessons I have learned from all these things as well as ask for guidance on the things I don't understand. This helps me become a better person. I do not learn just from victories; I also learn from defeat. I find direction not just from close to me, but also from those who oppose me. This helps me grow and be better. This is part of my life, and I hope it can become a part of others' lives.

Inspiration in life comes to all of us in different ways. For me, I find it in the books I read, the people I meet, the lessons I learn, and even in a flower I touch. I am honored by the smiles others share with me, and I am inquisitive about those that don't greet me with kindness. This is a journey. To be what I am meant to be, I must take every part of what I understand or don't understand and weave my spirit between the two worlds.

This is a way I am special. I see things differently. But YOU are special too. We are here to learn from one another, so let's do this by inspiring one another. I hope this book helps you find inspiration in the parts you understand, but I also hope it helps you question the parts of the book you don't understand. We aren't meant to understand everything. Yet we are meant to question everything; this is known as critical thinking.

Join me on this journey. You won't always agree with me, but we can agree to disagree and inspire one another because of our differences. It isn't the color of our skin or religion that causes so many divisive issues in this world. It is the fact that we haven't accepted that we are each part of one another. WE are each different because that is how it is supposed to be. I hope this book helps you see yourself in others as much as it helps you not see a bit of yourself in some people. I don't understand how I am like a blade of grass, except that I do understand that it feels the wind, and I do too. I spent an entire day once trying to imagine how the grass felt and how the wind made it happy, while also trying to understand how sad it was when the winter cold and ice made it wither. I wanted to understand the sadness so I could be more appreciative. I wanted to understand its joy and pain. I know that sounds silly, but is it really? We now know that rats feel empathy. We know sheep can count numbers. We know some dogs can communicate through a rudimentary form of sign language. They can even express anger or show when they are frustrated. These are facts we have uncovered as scientists. Can you imagine what we will someday know about how our flowers feel and think?

It is time to wake up. WE must cherish every minute we have on this earth. At the same time, we must cherish everything around us.

CHAPTER 1

Meeting with Yourself

When you first read this chapter's title, what thoughts came to mind? The reasons for meeting with yourself can be just as wide-ranging and diverse as meeting with other people.

Everyone needs to be genuine. Instead of being a submissive follower of social norms, you must be consistent with yourself. You need to "go on with your best life," pursuing your unique desires rather than adhering to what other people deem to be necessary for happiness. Studies have even demonstrated how feelings of validity can remain closely connected with various mental and social advantages: higher self-regard, more prominent wealth, better close connections, and improved work performance.

Yet authenticity carries some risk. Most people would define authenticity as acting in accordance with their individual set of values and characteristics. However, research has shown that people feel most credible when conforming to a specific understanding of socially endorsed characteristics, such as being extroverted, stable, reliable, faithful, scholarly, and pleasant.

The drawback of authenticity is that you might need to reveal your genuine nature in order to feel true. A person is deemed real from a psychological perspective if they satisfy certain requirements. Sincere people are driven to learn more about themselves and have a wealth of self-knowledge. They are equally interested in identifying their strengths and weaknesses, and they have the capacity to honestly examine feedback, whether favorable or unfavorable.

Most significantly, genuine individuals behave in accordance with their better qualities and characteristics, regardless of whether such eccentricities cause them to struggle with social pressures or other external influences. For instance, withdrawn people are genuine when they are quiet at a gathering, even though social etiquette dictates that they should participate in conversation.

Even as adults, our childhood habits continue to influence us. When you're older, it's likely you won't be doing something if you were punished or prevented from doing it when you were younger.

Monitoring one's attributes, behaviors, and emotions are all examples of maintaining self-awareness. It is a mental state in which one's self becomes the focal point of one's thoughts.

Possibly the first aspect of the idea of the self to emerge is self-awareness. While self-awareness is fundamental to your identity, it isn't something you intensely focus on every moment of the day. All things considered, self-awareness permeates the fabric of your identity and manifests itself in a variety of ways, depending on the circumstance and your personality. It involves giving back and paying attention to your thoughts and feelings as they develop. It tends to start with an understanding of the emotions you feel when spending time with specific people, or the thoughts that go through your mind when you are fearful of trying anything new. It is also a more complex, multilayered understanding of how your thoughts influence your feelings, behaviors, and emotions. For example, imagine yourself being unmotivated and having a lackluster outlook on the day ahead. Your energy may be low, and your body may feel heavy, which could cause you to stay in bed later than anticipated. At that point, you may start to think about how stuck you are and how difficult the day will be.

Infants do not have self-awareness at birth. However, research has found that children have a simple sense of awareness and self-appreciation. Infants exhibit behaviors that demonstrate their awareness of their independence from others. For instance, a newborn has an instinctive reflex to search for an areola when something brushes against their face. Specialists have additionally observed that even newborns can differentiate between self- and non-self-touch.

Self-consciousness is an exaggerated awareness of oneself, becoming preoccupied with oneself, especially how others might perceive one's looks or actions. Although self-consciousness and self-awareness are frequently used as swappable terms, they are not the same thing. Self-awareness refers to the state of being aware of one's independence or character, as well as different aspects of the self, such as feelings, characteristics, and desires. Self-awareness is many times thought about as a positive quality. Being aware of oneself as a person helps one fit in better, function normally in public, and maintain relationships.

Self-consciousness, to a degree, has some of the advantages of self-awareness. Self-consciousness is typically being overly conscious or worried about one's appearance or actions, which can be an issue now and again. Self-consciousness is frequently connected with an upsetting feeling, in contrast to self-awareness. Having the perception that "everyone is looking" might make one feel self-conscious because you feel seen, noticed, or judged. Some people are more self-conscious than others and can have related undesirable feelings as a result. Being self-conscious can bring about bashfulness, low self-regard, diminished confidence, jealousy, anxiety, depression, or paranoia.

What Should You Do to ENHANCE Your Awareness?

You may practice many techniques for raising awareness in your regular day-to-day activities, such as spending time in nature, meditating, keeping a journal, observing people, or just doing nothing (see below).

Nature plays a significant role in our spiritual lives. Despite the benefits, present-day life is disengaging us from this source of calm, motivation, concentration, and consciousness. If you wish to regularly experience this energy, you should consider investing some time every day or week focusing on nature as if it were as necessary as work.

If you want to meditate outdoors, you might try to calm your eyes by staring at a particular area without focusing on anything in particular, instead completely embracing the view.

Additionally, you may take a step further and use philosophical thinking to consider different properties of nature. For instance, if you're sitting by a river, you might notice it and move away. When you think back, is it still an unchanged stream? If a tree falls down in the forest you're walking through, and you didn't see it, did it fall? Whatever your question, attempt to consider it as profoundly as possible and elaborate on the response.

By observing nature, you may better comprehend your feelings and thoughts as well as feel more connected to the environment and the world around you. While learning about its varied qualities, it can be helpful to attempt to put what you have discovered into words.

It's normal to wish to transform your life through bettering yourself. You might be wondering how the journey of self-change starts.

Human beings have a complex relationship with change. While it is unavoidable and fundamental for development, change can likewise be profoundly uncomfortable—particularly if it feels involuntary or beyond our control.

The goal of human development is to never stop. As a matter of fact, no living thing on earth is intended to stop growing. We are continually moving toward the light as long as we are alive.

Progress in life is about reevaluation. Reevaluation is not the same thing as always seeking rewards or accomplishments. There is a difference, because success usually means an "end," where you achieve the objective and are "done." When you say,

"I'm done," it means you've stopped extending yourself, which implies you have quit developing.

Even after reevaluation, the conclusion is left open, which is something to be thankful for. Honest self-reflection gives you vast opportunities to keep exploring new pieces of yourself. This kind of development is internal rather than external, and exploration is development.

Whenever you find something important you need to change, search for a way to rethink it.

1. Observe yourself.

Imagine you are a sculptor. When a sculptor looks at a piece of stone, they are always thinking of better ways to shape it. Also, even if the sculptor thinks something needs to change, there is no personal connection. They do what needs to be done. This is how you want to see yourself, as a work of art. Don't bother getting upset or being hard on yourself when you see something you'd like to change. Get out your chisel and start working like an artisan.

2. Find the underlying causes of what you need to change.

People frequently focus more on what they need to change rather than the reasons that led to the problem in the first place. For instance, they may exercise, focusing excessively on their abdominal muscles in an effort to lose weight, despite the fact that their poor eating habits are the real cause of their weight issues. One must first recognize the patterns of behavior that gave rise to the tendency in the first place in order to properly reconsider changing aspects of oneself.

3. Practice consistently, come what may.

Change isn't something you implement for a short time. Committing today then taking a break tomorrow does not move you forward. A lifestyle change needs daily dedication until a new habit replaces an old one and doesn't require conscious effort.

4. Set logical goals for yourself.

You can't simply get up one morning and declare, "I won't be anxious anymore!" Quite frankly, yes, you will be. It can help to remember that no pattern of behavior will go away overnight.

All things being equal, make a goal to be more understanding during your personal reevaluation each day. Use that as a small place to practice and a subtle reminder of what you need to improve. Focus on that for two weeks and go from there.

5. Continually search in the mirror.

Things get problematic when you refuse to stop and look in the mirror or avoid self-reflection. There is a time and place for action, followed by an appropriate setting for reflection. Each is essential. Furthermore, if it takes effort to ask these challenging questions of yourself, you will quickly discover that you will veer off-course and be unsure how you got there.

6. Surround yourself with people who will be honest with you.

The company you keep is crucial to your progress. Surround yourself with people who help you progress, instead of those who continue to enable the behavior you want to change. You definitely want folks who won't hesitate to be honest with you and who will challenge your thinking. Truthful input is fundamental for self-improvement.

7. Face challenges head-on.

You won't become the individual you need to be by continuing to be who you are now. Growth requires you to get out of your comfort zone. It's challenging to take on things that are difficult and venture into the unknown. Furthermore, if you choose what's easy over what's hard, you will be in the same situation as before—curious, but afraid to take the risk.

A mental block is a restricting mindset that keeps you from finishing essential responsibilities and making progress. Mental blocks can be hard to detect, but these barriers disrupt the general flow of your efficiency.

Usually, mental barriers occur when we are distracted by our opinions. We might feel so overwhelmed or restless about a project's outcome that we are unable to do the necessary work. Your mental state while working frequently can be a great indicator of a mental block. Do you consider yourself to be unproductive, short-tempered, or incapable of eating or sleeping? If left unchecked, mental obstacles can have long-term effects, leading to fatigue and possibly affecting your ability to keep going in the future.

Do you frequently struggle to find the most effective way to get over a mental block? Everybody eventually faces a mental barrier in their lives; it doesn't just happen to experts or creatives. The qualities that allow us to perform at our finest and most productive levels—ingenuity, motivation, and clarity—are completely lacking.

There are many factors that might cause us to arrive at an impasse, especially at work. Being overwhelmed, a negative work environment, multitasking, or missed deadlines can all bring you to a total stop. When that happens, our internal growth halts, and we are unable to move on because we lack the necessary understanding to make a decision or imagine a course of action.

Sadly, there are no supernatural solutions that can break a performance impasse. However, we can rely on a few tried-and-true tricks to get through a mental obstacle. Not all of these tricks are appropriate for certain blockages or can be used out of the blue. Nonetheless, it's a good idea to have them on hand on the off-chance that your mind gets stuck like a vehicle in mud.

Certain states of mind or lack of self-esteem may create obstacles in people's lives. The following tips might help you to better understand why mental blocks occur and how to overcome them. The road to successful growth is ever-changing. It requires a long journey and is filled with both highs and lows.

1. Self-doubt

How many times have you put things off or delayed a fantastic idea because you weren't sure how it would turn out? Are there events from the past that keep you from engaging with others out of fear of rejection? Your current situation should serve as your greatest source of motivation, and your past shouldn't dictate your future. Don't allow who you used to be to prevent you from becoming who you can be.

2. Comparison

You draw contrasts between yourself and everyone and everything. The fact is, there are plenty of opportunities for everyone to win. For example, burgers can be sold by anyone, but what makes your burger stand unique are your management skills and special sauce. Comparing yourself to others will keep you in a state of frenzy and encourage you to follow the crowd rather than stand out.

3. Restricted mindset

You might look at the present and not think or plan for the future. You put stock in a bunch of patterns you have experienced in the past. However, circumstances are constantly changing. What you used last year might not be the best option right now. Be willing to accept new ideas, and work on groundbreaking thoughts and new strategies.

4. Lack of focus

Lack of focus is normal. We have all experienced it. This block appears to be caused by the way we frequently try to do too many things at once, becoming so busy that we lose sight of what is truly important. Imagine you decide to pursue one extraordinary thought and push it more consistently. What might that look like for you?

5. Sitting tight for the perfect moment

An ideal way to make a move is to begin simply. We can challenge ourselves by overanalyzing and overthinking, or we can follow our instincts and improvise with what we already have and know. On your journey, you will come to the realization that many people, companions, or even family members won't support you. It's okay to move forward single-handedly and pursue your vision alone. The vision is yours, not theirs, so continue to use your gifts and talents consistently to succeed.

6. Thinking you are not worthy of money

It's vital to recognize that you are the person who is preventing you from bringing in the money you need. Perhaps you grew up with practically zero income in your family. Maybe your folks burned through money and were barely able to provide for food, clothing, and a roof over your head. It might have encouraged a negative correlation and made you develop a naive money philosophy in which you believe that asking for more money is a serious issue. Therefore, you are reluctant to request a raise. Request more money for your efforts and accept that having more money will create more options. How we deal with the money affects our prosperity.

A successful person isn't someone with one primary resource but one with a prosperous mindset. Begin today by taking responsibility for your thoughts and emotions; build that mindset. Know that you are equipped to accomplish your objectives.

If your passion is to create a successful business or to accomplish something extraordinary in this world, then go get it. Although our minds were designed to make us feel safe, we occasionally overprotect ourselves and put our success on hold.

CHAPTER 2

Cracking the Shell

Our past experiences play an essential role in forming the individuals we are today. We are shaped by experiences and relationships from our youth with family and caregivers. A portion of these previous experiences can help to calm the anxious mind, which keeps us attached to the past, especially to negative experiences and feelings of hatred. Unsettled negative experiences from our past can definitely impact how we feel, think, and decide to act in the world today.

We go through opportunities for growth that help us become more joyful. However, we can also be left damaged by misfortunes, betrayals, and second thoughts. In fact, if you can't let go of the past, you'll find it difficult to give the future the attention it deserves, and you'll miss out on the joy of appreciating the present moment.

We have random reminders of past failures: A great concept that failed, sincere attempts that didn't pan out, or situations when unforeseen events derailed our intentions. In any case, making peace with your past will encourage you to go forward, gain knowledge from your experiences, and apply what you learned to live the greatest life possible.

Here's why you should choose to make peace with your past instead of attempting to fix it: Your unconscious mind safeguards traumatic memories and even shields them from being mended. This most likely sounds counterproductive, yet the main job of the unconscious mind is to keep you alive. So as hard as you try, you can't fix these painful memories, because the unconscious mind is documenting them regardless of whether you need them.

You Constantly Hide That You're Hurt

It tends to be difficult to hide that we're hurt. Maybe we feel our pain implies weakness on our part. Or we think feeling hurt so long after something happened suggests we have a neurosis or instability of some sort.

The reality is that if you feel hurt, you feel pain. Ignoring that pain won't make it disappear; it simply means you eventually will not have the option to control its impact on your life.

When you're at gatherings and telling horrible stories from the past to friends, do you feel compelled to share in what capacity it hurt you? Do you find yourself unable to trust and associate with individuals for reasons you don't even understand yourself? When you consider your past, do you characterize it by the times others have hurt you?

Once you have identified your pain, allow yourself to experience it. No matter how senseless or humiliating the feelings are, let yourself feel them completely. In most cases, painful feelings are trying to tell you something, and you can't move forward unless you accept their reality.

Allowing yourself to experience your feelings is pretty straightforward: simply sit down and monitor your body. If you feel miserable, where do you feel it? In your chest? Your arms and legs? Explore these sensations, and as you do, observe any reasons that arise that prevent you from putting a stop to these thoughts.

Contextualize Your Hurt

When you understand you're hurt, you'll want to accomplish the difficult work of contextualizing that hurt. To contextualize your hurt means to think once again about the past and see what happened with clear eyes. It implies that assuming your friends mistreated you, an ex controlled you, or a friend abandoned you, this says significantly more about them than you.

Many people who wind up tormented by the past are not contextualizing their hurt. They cling to it, making it more complex as the structure blocks for as long as they can remember the story. A few signs you are not contextualizing your past correctly include the following:

- You permit these hurts to fuel beliefs about yourself— for example, "I am broken," "I am damaged," or "I am detestable."
- No matter what you accomplish in different aspects of your life, it never appears to compensate for the awfulness of your past.

- The present feels unfilled and insignificant, and the past feels somehow more genuine.

If this is you, what you want to do is seriously investigate what occurred and recognize the truth about it. If a couple of years ago you fell into the arms of a manipulative man, you want to acknowledge that you never deserved his treatment. If a companion ghosted you, it expresses more about her shortcomings than your worthiness.

When you've appropriately contextualized your past, you'll start to feel a weight lifting off your shoulders. Rather than viewing yourself as terrible, unworthy, or awful, you'll see yourself as a normal person to whom a few terrible things have happened.

Forgive the People Who Hurt You

Forgiveness does not mean forgetting or becoming friends with the offender. To forgive, according to the American Heritage Dictionary, signifies "to repudiate anger or disdain." If you want to bury the hatchet on your past, you need to stop feeling angry at the people who hurt you.

That might mean controlling your anger against an ex who mistreated you. It might mean controlling your anger against your parents, who raised you poorly. It might also mean controlling your anger against yourself for doing something stupid and getting yourself mixed up with a wreck. Anything that it was, whoever it was, let go of your anger.

Forgiveness doesn't have anything to do with whether they understand they messed up or whether they "deserve" forgiveness. Holding anger and hurt in our bodies doesn't make the people who hurt us any sorrier. It does hurt us significantly more.

Furthermore, assuming you're holding on until the other individual sees the error of their ways—forget it. The simple fact of the matter is that many individuals who hurt you will never feel sorry, particularly people who hurt you the most. Many people will feel churlish and reluctant to apologize, insist they did nothing out of line, or even forget that anything ever happened. If you wait for other individuals to do the self-improvement essential for them to acknowledge your experience, you'll be waiting forever. It's as simple as that.

The process of putting the past behind you isn't simple. You might feel back to your standard self for a few days, only to find different days are weighed down by the heaviness of what's occurred. This is normal and doesn't have to be a problem. Healing is an unsure and lopsided process, yet you will arrive in the long run, assuming you stay with it. We all will.

Think about a time when you were contemplating a significant decision at work or considering a major expense like a house, a large financial investment, or the establishment of a new business. Such choices are innately complex, and regardless of how much experience we have making them, dealing with the advantages and disadvantages of every decision can be overpowering. Our emotional responses to these choices may aid in focusing our thoughts and energies on what we perceive to be the main aspects of the decision. Deep emotions, though, could push us to make unwise or downright depressing decisions.

We need to experience this essential transformation to ready ourselves for the next situation. It's just like changing from a fertilized egg into a baby in the womb in anticipation of this world.

The best and most significant adventure of our lives is finding out who we are. On the other hand, a significant number of us live our lives without being aware of who we are. Too often, we fall prey to a nasty inner voice that bombards us with every single one of these unacceptable thoughts about ourselves. We mistakenly think of self-understanding as self-indulgence, and we carry on without asking the most important question we'll ever ask: Who am I truly? Or as Mary Oliver put it, "How is it you plan to manage your one wild and valuable life?"

Finding yourself might seem like an intrinsically narcissistic goal. However, an unselfish process is at the foundation of everything we do throughout everyday life. To be the most significant individual in our surroundings—the best partner, parent, and so on—we need to know what our identity is, what we value, and as a result, what we bring to the table. This individual journey is one everyone will benefit from taking. The process includes separating—shedding layers that don't serve us or reflect who we truly are. However, it also includes a significant demonstration of evolving—understanding who we need to be and actively working toward fulfilling our unique predetermination, whatever that may be. It involves understanding our power while remaining receptive and open to our experiences.

It isn't something to avoid at all costs or to be afraid of; rather, we should look at it with the same curiosity and compassion we would show toward an intriguing new companion. In light of these criteria, the steps that will be discussed in the following paragraphs are considered to be the most beneficial along this extremely personal journey.

Excruciating experiences from our past are valuable, as they frequently decide how we characterize and protect ourselves. To put it plainly, they twist us, influencing our conduct in ways we are not aware. For instance, having a brutal parent might have made us feel more guarded. We might grow up continuously feeling on guard or unable to attempt new challenges because of a paranoid fear of being disparaged. It's easy to see how carrying this fragility into adulthood could undermine our sense of self and cause us to falter in a number of areas. To break this example of conduct, it's significant to recognize what's driving it. We need to constantly look for where our most narrow-minded or foolish tendencies come from.

We may suffer disorientation and a lack of familiarity with ourselves whenever we try to hide or ignore our past experiences. We might take action naturally without inquiring as to why. By participating in this sort of thinking and being willing to confront the recollections that emerge, we gain priceless experiences in our way of behaving. After that, we may start to consciously separate the negative effects of our experiences and make changes to our conduct that represent how we honestly think and believe as well as how we choose to be in society.

1. **Differentiate.**

The term *differentiation* refers to the act of working to cultivate within ourselves the feeling that we are free people. To be ourselves and satisfy our one-of-a-kind preferences, we should separate from disastrous relational, familial, and cultural impacts that don't serve us. According to Dr. Robert Firestone, "To have a free existence, an individual should isolate him/herself from negative influence and stay open and vulnerable." In his work with many people struggling with this process, he created four fundamental stages of differentiation:

- Step 1: Break with harmful internalized thought processes, i.e., critical, hostile attitudes toward self and others.
- Step 2: Separate from negative personality traits assimilated from one's parents.
- Step 3: Relinquish patterns of defense formed as an adaptation to painful events in one's childhood.
- Step 4: Develop one's own values, ideals, and beliefs rather than automatically accepting those one has grown up with.

In order to find ourselves, we must all seek out our sense of purpose. This means splitting our perspective from others' expectations of us. It suggests identifying our strengths and what matters most to us, after which we should act in accordance with the values we hold dear. It concentrates on showing that the most optimistic individuals search out the importance of something other than fun and that individuals are happier when they have goals that reach out past themselves. Therefore, finding yourself and your happiness is an effort inseparably connected to finding meaning.

2. Think about what you need.

There's a tendency in life to focus on the negative. Instead of placing ourselves toward more uplifting objectives, tactics, and principles, many individuals find it much too easy to sink into negative thoughts and complaints about our situations and the external variables that surround us. Simply put, we think a great deal about what we don't need instead of focusing on what we do.

Knowing what we need is key to finding ourselves. Understanding our needs and desires aids in our understanding of who we are and what is important to us. This might sound basic, yet most of us are to varying degrees protected against our feelings of need. We can't get hurt, so we feel a sense of security. Having a need for certain things makes us feel both alive and vulnerable in our place in the world. To genuinely live means we can lose. The experience of happiness and satisfaction can be met with feelings of fear and, on a deeper level, pain.

Getting what we need can likewise cause us to feel awkward because it causes a break from before. It can cause us to feel remorse or be overcome by a barrage of negative self-talk that tells us, "Who do you think you are? You can't find success/fall in love/feel free." To genuinely find what we need throughout everyday life, we should silence this inward critic and drop our defenses. As an exercise, when we have many negative thoughts such as "I don't need anything," we can attempt to position our thinking to what we truly want. If we are battling with our partner and think, "You never hear what I say. You couldn't care less about me," we can instead think about or even describe our thoughts on a level that truly conveys our ultimate objective: "I need to feel paid attention to, be seen, and be adored." Changing our perspective in this way causes us to feel more in touch with what our identity is. It deprives us of our most fundamental desires without the pointless layers of defense that redirect us from our basic beliefs and most genuine selves.

3. Perceive your personal power.

When we know what we need, we are called to come into our own power. Never again should we take part in twisted, negative thinking that lets us know everything that matters with our general surroundings or every one of the reasons we can't have what we need. All things being equal, we tolerate ourselves as powerful players in our fate, and coming into our personal power is fundamental for finding and becoming ourselves.

Personal power depends on the strength, certainty and ability people gain over everyday turns of events, step by step. It is self-attestation and a characteristic, a solid taking a stab at affection, fulfillment, and importance in one's interpersonal world. Knowing our power means perceiving that we intensely affect our lives. We make the world we live in. To create a better society, we must change our perspective, feel confident in doing so, and reject an oppressed viewpoint.

Dr. Firestone has outlined "Six Aspects of Being an Adult":

- Experience your feelings yet go with informed choices regarding how you act.

- Figure out goals and make the right moves to accomplish them.
- Be proactive and self-decisive, as opposed to uninvolved and subordinate.
- Look for balance in your connections.
- Be available to explore novel thoughts and welcome useful criticism.
- Take full power over all aspects of your conscious reality.

4. Know the worth of friendship.

We don't pick the family we are born into, yet frequently we accept that this family characterizes our identity. As children, we have little say in where we invest our energy, but we can pick who and what we need to emulate all through our lives. As grown-ups, we can make a group of decisions. We may discover people who satisfy us, who support what enlightens us, and who inspire us to have a positive outlook on our lives. This family may include people with whom we are acquainted, but it's a core group we have chosen and who we consider to be obvious partners and companions. Making this family is a critical part of finding ourselves, since who we decide to surround ourselves with significantly affects how we relate to life. Having an emotional support network that has faith in us helps us understand our goals and create on a personal level.

CHAPTER 3

The Gems Who Defied All the Odds

Kintsugi is the Japanese art of putting broken pottery back together with gold, based on the idea that you can create a much stronger, more attractive piece of art by embracing flaws and defects. Each break is unique, and as a part of fixing an object like new, the four-hundred-year-old procedure features the "scars" as a part of the plan. Using this as an analogy for healing ourselves shows us a significant example: Sometimes, when we fix things that are broken, we create something more unique, lovely, and resilient.

There are many "kintsugi people" who have set an example for us in history. Despite being flawed, they have given their best, setting an example for generations to come. In this chapter, we will discuss what it is like to be one of these people.

The people we study in history books are successful because of their growth. This doesn't mean simple aging but implies growth from past experiences and traumas.

It has been discovered that negative experiences can produce positive change, including realizing one's own strength, exploring new opportunities, forming relationships, having a more obvious respect for everything, and experiencing profound growth. We see this in individuals who have gotten through war, cataclysmic events, deprivation, employment trouble, financial stress, complex conditions, and wounds. So, despite the hopelessness coming about because of the COVID pandemic, large numbers of us can hope to improve our lives in its aftermath. Furthermore, leaders can help other people to do the same.

Even though post-traumatic growth frequently happens without psychotherapy or other intervention, it may be worked with in five ways: education, emotional development, communication, relationship building, and self-management. As a matter of fact, numerous people who experience injury—for example, being diagnosed with an ongoing or terminal illness, losing a friend or family member, or being assaulted—show staggering strength and flourishing in the repercussions of the awful incident. Studies show that most injury survivors don't foster PTSD. A huge number even report growth from their experience. Richard Tedeschi and Lawrence Calhoun coined the term "post-traumatic growth" to capture this peculiarity, characterizing it as the positive mental change experienced by the struggle with challenging life circumstances.

These seven areas of growth have been reported to spring from adversity:

- Greater appreciation of life
- Greater appreciation and strengthening of close relationships

- Increased compassion and altruism
- The identification of new possibilities or a purpose in life
- Greater awareness and utilization of personal strengths
- Enhanced spiritual development
- Creative growth

Undoubtedly, the vast majority who experience post-traumatic growth would prefer not to have had the trauma, and not many of these situations show more growth after trauma as opposed to sharing positive educational experiences. The great majority of people who go through post-traumatic growth are usually shocked by it, and it frequently occurs unexpectedly as a result of an effort to make sense of an incomprehensible experience.

In fact, many of the strategies for recovering from trauma conflict with our natural tendencies to avoid uncomfortable feelings and thoughts.

Even so, the only way we can start to accept the unavoidable facts of life and get a more nuanced view of the world around us is to give up the natural protections we have in place to keep us safe, face our situation head-on, and see everything we go through as information for our own growth.

After a traumatic event, whether a chronic illness or the death of a family member or a good friend, it's natural to stew over the event, continually contemplating what occurred, replaying the thoughts and feelings again and again. This is in many cases a sign that you are working hard to sort out what happened, effectively destroying old belief systems and creating new models of importance and identity.

While rumination typically starts as programmed, intrusive, and redundant, after some time such reasoning turns out to be more organized, controlled and purposeful. This course of change can be horrendous. Yet rumination related to painful areas of strength for an emotionally supportive network and different sources for articulation may aid in our development and give us the capacity to access deep reservoirs of empathy and cooperation we didn't even know we had.

Similarly, emotions such as distress, despair, anger, and anxiety are normal reactions to trauma. Rather than doing all we can to restrain or "self-manage" those emotions, experiential evasion by staying away from dreaded thoughts, feelings, and sensations strangely compounds the situation, building up our conviction that the world isn't safe and making it more challenging to seek cherished long-term objectives. Through avoiding experiences, we shut down our exploratory limits along these lines, passing up numerous open doors for producing positive experiences and significance. This is a central topic of acknowledgment and responsibility treatment (ACT), which assists individuals with expanding their "mental adaptability." By adopting mental flexibility, we approach the world with curiosity and transparency. We are better ready to respond to events with the help of our established values.

Some people have hearing, speech, and vision impairments. Others have physical and mental disabilities. People who are debilitated are those who have been seriously injured, such as those who are handicapped, visually impaired, or nonverbal, as well as those who have some kind of physical deformities. Most of the time, they are at the mercy of other people. Those who are intellectually disabled sometimes struggle with the negative impacts of mental conditions such as cerebral paralysis and Down syndrome, amongst other conditions. They see themselves as the burden of their family, and as long as they are alive, they constantly feel inadequate.

We also cannot forget the people who have not only set an example by growth but have also shown us how to live with a disability and not let it affect their life goals.

"Disability should not be an obstacle to progress," Stephen Hawking wrote in the first World Disability Report in 2011. There are many disabled people in Asia, and many face segregation consistently, which takes many forms.

Many managers recruit disabled individuals as a last option, as it is viewed more as a responsibility than a resource to the company. Nonetheless, these fears are totally unwarranted. Individuals with actual disabilities are not a dismissible class of individuals. Many visually impaired and hearing-debilitated people have contributed massively to organizations they belong to. As a matter of fact, there are many instances of how disabled people have been successful working for themselves. In addition to those who have become professors and specialists through pure hard work and perseverance, their examples of overcoming adversity are remembered by others who know how to run their own businesses, such as shops, restaurants, and handicraft centers. Many have even become effective sportspersons, taking part in the Paralympics Games and dominating the medal board. It has been demonstrated that those with a disabled frame of mind can't handle blooming into a superstar.

As indicated by the UN Convention on the Rights of Persons with Disabilities, almost 15 percent of the total populace lives with a disability of some sort. Surprisingly, however, only 160 countries have signed the agreement; something like 20 nations, including the United States, have not confirmed the arrangement. It comes down to the fact that despite perceiving the need to build a comprehensive society where individuals with disabilities have equivalent opportunities, numerous nations are yet to follow up on it. In any case, such hurdles only sometimes influence the most driven individuals.

Helen Keller

Helen Adams Keller was born healthy in the United States in 1880. An illness left her both deaf and blind before the age of two. The organizations accessible to individuals with inabilities are, without a doubt, less than impressive today. Yet the circumstances in those days were much worse. Notwithstanding the challenges, Keller's mom believed her girl should get the best education and searched for specialists who could assist her with accomplishing that.

Keller attended Radcliffe College in Cambridge, Massachusetts, and graduated in 1904 with a four-year expression certification, being the first deaf-blind person to do so. During her time at the college, her correspondence with the Austrian rationalist Wilhelm Jerusalem assisted him with finding her scholarly abilities and denoted the start of Keller's profession as an essayist and a social lobbyist. She rose to prominence as an advocate for people with disabilities and gained global recognition for her writings and speeches on topics as diverse as communism and contraception.

Stephen Hawking

Born in 1942 in Oxford, England, Stephen William Hawking is one of the most acclaimed personalities of the twenty-first century. He has been a theoretical physicist, cosmologist, creator, director of research at the Center for Theoretical Cosmology at the University of Cambridge, an honorary Fellow of the Royal Society of Arts, and a lifetime member of the Pontifical Academy of Sciences.

In 1963, at twenty-one years old, Hawking was diagnosed with a slow-growing type of amyotrophic horizontal sclerosis (ALS), otherwise called motor neuron disease. At that point, his PCPs accepted he wouldn't live longer than two more years. However, Hawking surprised them all and proceeded with his work as a researcher and an excellent example for individuals with disabilities all over the planet.

Srikanth Bolla

Srikanth Bolla was born in 1992 into a farming family in Seetharamapuram, a seaside city in the Andhra Pradesh region of India. A few neighbors even encouraged his unfortunate guardians to cover him and save themselves from the aggravation of dealing with a youngster brought into the world without eyes. When he arrived at secondary school, he was not allowed to concentrate on science and had to fight a six-month-long court battle. Afterward, he was denied a chance to learn at the Indian Institute of Technology even though he had scored 98 percent on their entrance exam.

Despite the chances, Srikanth Bolla never surrendered, and he proceeded to become the first blind student to learn at the Massachusetts Institute of Technology and procure a science certification as he had consistently longed for. After finishing his investigations, Bolla returned to India and started a business in his home state. Today his organization, Bollant Industries, has an estimated worth of over INR 500 million ($6.1 million USD) and employs many individuals with disabilities.

Sai Kaustuv Dasgupta

Twenty-six-year-old Sai Kaustuv Dasgupta was diagnosed with osteogenesis imperfecta, otherwise called "Fragile Bone Disease." Because of this condition, he has experienced over fifty broken bones up to this point, and he is dependent on a motorized wheelchair to move around. His family moved from their old neighborhood, Siliguri in West Bengal, to Puttaparthi in Andhra Pradesh, when he was just two years of age. Sai was totally out of commission between 2009 and 2015 after his health weakened.

None of this hindered him from becoming a very effective artworks creator, vocalist and music composer, writer, and powerful speaker. Sai has previously won many honors and received acknowledgment for his work all over the planet. His book has been interpreted into six languages, and he has traveled to numerous nations all over the globe. A trip to Siliguri is high on his list of priorities, despite the fact that he has never been able to visit his old neighborhood due to the lack of accessible mobility options.

Ralph Braun

Ralph Braun was just a young child when he was diagnosed with muscular dystrophy, a group of genetic diseases that produces a deficiency of muscle mass.

A couple of years after his diagnosis, Ralph started to lose his ability to walk. While experts cautioned him that he might never be capable of living independently, the young boy defied expectations by building the first battery-operated bike. His drive finally inspired him to found the wheelchair manufacturer BraunAbility.

He passed on in 2013, yet as his organization's website notes, his heritage lives on: "Need is the mother of development. Ralph's actual limits simply energized his assurance to live freely and demonstrate to society that individuals with actual inabilities can partake completely and effectively throughout everyday life."

Frida Kahlo

Mexico's most well-known artist, Frida Kahlo, was born with spina bifida, which can cause defects in the spinal cord. At six, she contracted polio, which made one leg thinner than the other.

Notwithstanding these challenges, she was a normal kid. However, at the age of 18, a car accident left her with real wounds. While recuperating from the mishap, Frida found her affection for painting. She would become one of the most well-known Surrealists on the planet.

J. K. Rowling

One of the best-selling authors in history is J. K. Rowling. However, Rowling's notoriety didn't come easily. She was a single parent living on government assistance, attempting to help her little girl. It took her seven years to compose the narrative of *Harry Potter and the Sorcerer's Stone*. Twelve significant publishing houses dismissed the book when she was done.

Walt Disney

Disney was fired as a young man from his work on the local newspaper for an absence of intelligent thoughts. Then, in 1921, he launched his first animation company, but it failed.

He wound up eating dog food to make do. Could you start another animation firm if you were surviving on dog food? Presumably not. In any case, that is precisely what Walt Disney did. He had to restart a few more times after that before finally becoming successful.

The Beatles

In the beginning, the Beatles were close to reaching every record milestone. In any case, they didn't stop, and the rest is history. They've sold over 1.6 billion albums and then some.

Colonel Harland Sanders

Colonel Harland Sanders was the organizer behind the Kentucky Fried Chicken (KFC) franchise. He flopped in practically every undertaking he engaged with throughout his whole life. Nevertheless, at the age of 65, he set out to sell chicken using his renowned secret recipe and just a $105 federal retirement support check. One thousand nine restaurants dismissed him before one accepted his deal.

Dr. Seuss

One of the most celebrated child authors ever is likewise possibly the most renowned disappointment. Theodore Geisel, known by his more famous pen-name Dr. Seuss, expected to earn his PhD in writing at Lincoln College, Oxford, yet fizzled and ultimately left the school. His first notable work, *And to Think I Saw It on Mulberry Street*, was rejected twenty-eight separate times. Be that as it may, he didn't surrender. By the time of his death in 1991, he had sold more than 600 million copies of his books in twenty distinct languages.

Jim Carrey

Jim Carrey is a comedic legend, yet he grew up very poor as a youngster. At fifteen years old, Carrey worked as a janitor to assist his family with covering the bills. During his most memorable exhibition at Yuk's, a satire club in Toronto, he was mocked on the stage.

Keanu Reeves

Keanu Reeves endured immense difficulties growing up. At three years old, his dad deserted his loved ones. His mom married and separated four times, moving him from Australia to Canada. He eventually wound up in Los Angeles. In 1998, his child was stillborn at eight months. A year and a half after their relationship ended, his ex was killed in an auto crash.

Tyler Perry

Perry had an unpleasant childhood. He was physically and sexually abused growing up, expelled from secondary school, and attempted suicide twice, once as an adolescent and again at age 22.

In 1992, he wrote, produced, and starred in his most memorable theater creation, *I Know I've Been Changed*, to some degree informed by his disturbing childhood. Perry put every ounce of his investment funds into the show. It was a pitiful failure; there was only one week of performances, and just thirty people attended. He stayed aware of the creation, working more unspecialized temp jobs, and frequently slept in his car to scrape by. After six years, Perry at long last got a breakthrough when, on its seventh run, the show turned into a triumph. He's since proceeded to have a very effective vocation as a chef, author, and entertainer. Perry was named *Forbes'* highest compensated man in entertainment in 2011.

Oprah Winfrey

Many people know Oprah as one of the most famous faces on TV and one of the most beloved ladies on the planet. Oprah faced a hard road to get to that position. She endured a rough and often abusive childhood and numerous career setbacks, including being fired from her job as a television reporter because she was "unfit for TV."

* * *

After you read their real-life stories, I'm pretty sure that these people's lives will motivate and encourage you to never give up and trust your journey. Life may get tough at times, but that does not mean it won't get better. It's often said, "When life gives you lemons, make lemonade." So don't give up. The opportunity to make a better life is yours.

CHAPTER 4

A New Dream with a Renewed Spirit

Trusting in yourself implies genuinely believing in your own abilities. It means having the option to trust yourself to do what you say you'll do and realizing that those efforts will bring about the ideal results. Having faith in yourself results from a few crucial psychological experiences: self-worth, self-confidence, self-trust, independence, and control over one's circumstances. Below, we'll go through how to build each of these aspects of yourself and why doing so can help you feel more confident in yourself.

When we have faith in ourselves, it starts a wide range of psychological cycles that assist us with accomplishing our goals, manifesting our dreams, and increasing our worth. Be that as it may, the other side is also obvious. The absence of self-confidence or lack of trust in ourselves implies we are more averse to acting, changing, or pushing to improve things. Therefore, when we hope to shine, we are bound to come up short.

That implies that trusting in ourselves is similar to the key that turns the ignition and starts the vehicle. We can't exactly go anywhere without it. Every time we try to propel ourselves forward, we're impeded because our thoughts, attitudes, and activities aren't aligned with our goals. So either we don't do what we want to do, or we sabotage ourselves along the way, in some cases intentionally, and at times in an unconscious manner.

Have Faith in Your Worth

The first and maybe most fundamental part of trusting in yourself is accepting that you have worth. Why would you strive to pursue your aspirations if you find it difficult to believe that you are deserving of them? On the other hand, on the off chance that you consider yourself likeable, this positive self-treatment can go far toward having faith in yourself.

We can begin to develop our self-worth by caring for ourselves and rehearsing skills such as self-empathy. When we struggle or make mistakes, we should have nice conversations with ourselves, advocate for ourselves, and relax. Positive affirmations could also be used to assist us in remembering the kind thoughts we need to have about ourselves.

Trust Your Good Qualities

To trust yourself, you should accept that you have the characteristics or skills necessary to do anything you need or want to do. How does that work? Making a list of your talents and good traits might be helpful in the beginning because you'll be able to identify them.

Then, think about how these positive characteristics and qualities can assist you with arriving at your goals. When you see precisely the number of good qualities you have and how they are helpful to you, then ideally you'll need to depend less on trust to put stock in yourself. At the very least, you'll see it directly before you—you will be able to say, "Yes! I'm a person who can achieve this objective!"

Additionally, if you happen to lack any of the crucial skills you need in order to achieve your goals, start working on developing them right now. Not a single one of us comes into this world having all we want to achieve all we need. So if there are still skills you need to develop, concentrate on how your current traits and attributes can help you do so. We develop gradually, increasing our self-confidence a little with each positive step we take.

Believe in Yourself by Building Self-Trust

We frequently consider trust to be something we have for other people. Be that as it may, we likewise have (or don't have) trust for ourselves. Having (or not having) this trust in ourselves has ramifications, such as having (or not having) trust for other people. For instance, when we trust somebody, we're straightforward with them, we can rely on them, and we are sure that they will help us when we need them.

So what does it mean when we lack faith in ourselves? Indeed, we would rather not be straightforward with ourselves since we don't know how we'll manage that information. Perhaps we can't rely on ourselves to carry out our promises to ourselves. Or, on the other hand, perhaps we're concerned about the likelihood that we'll cause more harm to ourselves instead of helping ourselves.

It might sound odd when explained this way. To be honest, though, a lot of us do struggle with self-trust issues. For instance, perhaps we have promised ourselves repeatedly that we will start exercising, but we never follow through. So what are the chances we'll believe ourselves when we again say we will work out? Not likely.

Or perhaps we've told ourselves repeatedly that we're in a cheerful marriage, yet in reality the marriage is crumbling. We've been deceiving ourselves. How might we then attempt to believe in ourselves? For this reason, building self-trust can be a crucial stage in having confidence in ourselves. We need to turn into a group that we can believe in.

Ways to Gain Self-Trust

Here are a few steps to begin building trust in yourself:

- Do what you say you will do. Perhaps this implies decreasing your number of responsibilities, figuring out how to say no, or adhering to a timetable. Try different techniques so you can best adhere to your promise.
- Be straightforward with yourself. Take part in self-reflection to get to the reality of your thought process, feelings, and needs throughout everyday life. In an effort to view yourself as you truly are, try to block out the "shoulds" of the world.

- Do what you believe is correct. Experience your own values and follow your inner compass. It'll probably be easier to have faith in your ability to follow that course if you're on a consistent path with yourself.
- Be clear. Be more specific about who you are and what you require. Know the things you will do and the things you won't. You can trust yourself to use sound judgment and convey your needs effectively.

Believe in Yourself by Cultivating Self-Empowerment

Independence is the potential for self-management. It is the chance we need to make our own decisions and pursue our unique strategies in daily life. It is also referred to as self-empowerment, which is the ability to take control of our lives, set our own priorities, and make our own choices. As a rule, we have independence to some degree in the U.S., yet there are many motivations behind why we might not feel like we have independence. We should discuss a couple of these.

How Our Job Can Damage Self-Empowerment

In relation to our jobs, we might feel like we lack independence because we must work at specific times, perform tasks we would rather avoid, and unfortunately allow others to make decisions for us. The more accustomed one becomes to this lack of empowerment, the more problematic it may be to feel self-enabled. We could start by asking ourselves: Can we make decisions on our own? Do we have influence and control over our lives? We have very little practice at it.

How Our Loved Ones Can Harm Self-Empowerment

Another way we could lose empowerment comes from our good-natured loved ones. Our parents in particular may advise us to pursue certain objectives or conduct our lives with a specific goal in mind. For example, perhaps they have told us that we ought to obtain a conventional job, get married, and have children by the time we are thirty years old.

The "shoulds" from our loved ones can frequently sabotage us. We probably won't feel like we truly have command over our lives because having that control could upset those we care about or change how they see us. In this situation, putting stock in ourselves could prompt circumstances that we're anxious about or cause us to feel awkward. Therefore, we might unwittingly choose not to believe in ourselves.

How Our Way of Life Can Hurt Self-Empowerment

Another aspect that regularly hurts self-empowerment is societal norms. We might not believe in ourselves if we desire to be president—for example, if we are a woman and no woman has ever held the office of president. The equivalent could be valid if we are a woman who desires to be a technician or another male-dominated profession. The same applies to men who need or desire to work in a female-dominated profession.

It can be challenging to have faith in your ability to do what others like you have not tried or accomplished. You might not feel as though you have true control over something that seems legitimate and is embodied by social powers beyond your reach.

Believe in Yourself by Reclaiming Your Power

These circumstances can remove a portion of our control and power. By investigating these circumstances, you can check whether any of these undermining encounters keep you from having confidence in yourself. Ask yourself whether there is a message you have been repeatedly told by your family, your culture, or your place of employment that is causing you to be uncertain.

Believe in Yourself by Learning to Master Your World

Investigating not just our history but also the conditions of our lives right now may be of great assistance in helping to get the results we are looking for. It is likely we will not possess the confidence in our abilities to accomplish our goals if we put in a valiant effort and still fail. Having failed previously further justifies the lack of confidence or willingness to try again.

Given the difficulty of the situation, we might be tempted to believe that our best efforts fall short. Why believe in ourselves—why attempt—when it doesn't appear to work?

In research, this type of phenomenon is sometimes referred to as "learned helplessness." Early research showed that when animals were repeatedly exposed to electric shocks, they stopped trying to get away even when circumstances changed and made it possible to do so (Maier & Seligman, 1976). They had learned from repeated failures that no matter what they did, they could not change their situation. They could not master their environment. As a result, they no longer believed in themselves.

The Most Effective Method to Master Your Reality

Several additional reputable studies examined techniques for reversing acquired helplessness but provided few clear answers. In general, it seems that setting modest, doable goals and moving on to bigger ones when able can help people reclaim a sense of ecological mastery. For instance, one review told older people the best way to develop and deal with a plant to support natural mastery. Simply the demonstration of assuming command over your current circumstance in some little way can help.

As a rule, we must take advantage of effective goal-setting procedures and be certain not to make excessively aggressive goals. Defining far-off goals may simply support the conviction that we cannot meet our goal or achieve the outcomes we want.

Seeking our dreams sounds magical and charming, and what's more, when we start pursuing our ambitions, it's a special experience for the majority of us. Everything is energizing, new, and fascinating, and the entire world is in front of us.

Yet accomplishing a dream is something different. Working can be demanding and occasionally discouraging. Additionally, it may take a very long time before we realize our aspirations.

The majority of people in our society and culture think we should believe we can achieve our dreams and end up in a magical place that is known for progress, where we can make a lot of money and live our dreams without limitation.

For most people, the truth is that they give up too soon or just short of reaching their goals. On the other hand, they might not know who they are and what they want out of life. Even more dreams are destroyed when the desire for the dream is stronger than the effort to make it happen.

It all begins with you. What defines you as a person and what matters to you are the first steps toward truly realizing your aspirations. You cannot realize your dreams if you do not have the slightest idea about these two things.

That being the case, how do we truly understand who we are and what we want out of life?

It starts as seeing yourself as someone who goes after their dreams and then finds a way to get them. What's more, once we have found our identity, we should focus on our needs and talk about our goals.

1. Create your identity.

Your beliefs, activities, and physical appearance all contribute to who you are. You can change this identity to reflect who you need to be in this life. Of course, it takes effort, just like everything else.

Ask yourself:

"What is it that I truly want? What kind of individual is responsible for making that happen?"

Take a little time and thoroughly consider these answers. When we start to truly understand these aspects of who we are, it will lead us to the next, most important step in achieving our goals.

2. Identify your priorities.

Your needs are vital to your dreams. On the off-chance they don't serve you, then at that point you will most likely not accomplish what you set out to do. Therefore, one of our primary goals is to identify our needs and ensure they are compatible with our sense of ourselves and our goals.

You have needs in four main areas: spiritual, personal, vocational, and actionable.

We build our lives around ourselves in these four areas: with our friends and families, our jobs, and the things we do in our spare time. If we put our professional ambitions ahead of our families in order to achieve the life we see for ourselves, our personal lives are less likely to thrive.

3. Clarify your dreams.

When we have defined who we are and what we need, we are finally able to articulate our goals and dreams. Explaining our dreams also requires understanding what is important to us—the things we really need in life.

These aren't things like another vehicle or the most recent iPhone, but things like traveling to the far corners of the planet, writing a book, living in your dream house, working at the most amazing job you could ever ask for, and so on.

Now that you have identified what you want, take it a step further and ask yourself, "What is my wildest dream?" After some evaluation, you may need to adjust your personality in order to make your aspirations come true.

When you have a strong grasp on who you are, and are aware of both your needs and dreams, the time is perfect to take the next step in realizing your goals. The decision must now be made of what path to take.

A Life Plan

We need a plan to get from where we are to where we are going. The ideal way to accomplish your dreams is by making a life plan. A life plan is a living narrative that evolves as you make progress toward your dreams and goals in life.

The significant thing about a life plan is that it compels you to recognize where you are, affirm your vision for the future, and wisely choose the steps you will take to get there.

Given that it covers all aspects of your life, the best method is to start charting a course toward achieving your goals. Every need in your life should be taken into account in a valid life plan, along with the future aspirations and desires associated with those needs.

Goal Setting

Recently, others have shared that creating goals is no longer a useful strategy to achieve their dreams. However, that couldn't be more wrong! Goal setting is an essential step in accomplishing our dreams. A large number of people choose goals that lack vision or, even worse, pick goals that are not their own, and this is what leads to the assumptions that goal setting itself is useless.

We have found that setting goals is a great way to get going in the right direction. When we have a plan for our lives, we want to reach certain goals along the way to our dreams.

We put forth goals in the context of setting the direction of our life plan. They are fueled by the vision we desire and the identity we have created to achieve our dreams.

Goal setting isn't intended to be the only step in accomplishing your dreams.

A System

What truly brings life planning and goal setting together is the right system to achieve those goals. Without a system, the decisions we make might never materialize. We often establish plans and declare our objectives, but for some reason we seldom follow through with them. Additionally, it makes people feel horrible when this happens.

However, when we have a system of questions and discussions where we evaluate our progress and adjust our course, we can achieve our goals, plans, and dreams.

Vision and direction are insufficient for making your dreams work out. When these two viewpoints are laid out, we should make a move. Without action, we won't achieve our dreams.

In any case, many people will do the initial segment and not take the necessary actions to MOVE toward their goals.

Our development comes as the following activities, behaviors, and habits.

Next Steps

When we initially head out to chase our dreams, we want to zero in on making the following moves. These are the little wins you can begin at any time. The best time is the present.

For the overwhelming majority of us, we want to get the energy moving before we can truly take a step toward our dreams. In this way, we want to begin by zeroing in on what we want to do next toward that aspiration.

These next activities are gradual steps to get you going in the correct direction. As we string a handful of these together, we start to create behaviors for pursuing our dreams.

Behaviors

As we set up a line of positive activities toward our goals, we see behaviors shaping—positive, dream-accomplishing behaviors. This is when the activity toward our dreams becomes more straightforward. What's more, we can add to them.

As we create new behaviors, it consolidates our new identity, and it assists us with advancing toward our dreams even more rapidly. Furthermore, our confidence develops.

When we become more confident in our ability to follow our dreams, we begin to make progress, achieve goals toward our objectives, and eventually succeed. Yet this doesn't happen until we have transformed our behaviors into habits.

Habits

When we define our habits, we see our goals and plans working as expected. Our habits assist with pushing us toward our dreams without knowing when or if they will come true.

As we focus on our habits, we begin to see routines developing. These habits are the result of our activities, which have transformed into behaviors and are presently important for our everyday lives.

These habits are programmed activities.

CHAPTER 5

Maintaining Physical, Mental, and Spiritual Well-Being

Physical fitness contributes to the protection and development of the endurance of a person's breathing, heart function, muscular strength, and shape. Regular exercise, adequate rest, and balanced nutrition all add to good health. People receive medical treatment to maintain the balance when necessary. Physical well-being involves having a healthy lifestyle to minimize the risk of disease.

Physical health can allude to an individual's physical activity level, diet, nutrition, sleep cycle, and level of use of alcohol or medications. Individuals with great physical health are likely to be in overall peak condition. This isn't simply due exclusively to a lack of disease. Normal activity, balanced nutrition, and sufficient rest add to excellent health, and individuals get clinical treatment to keep up with the balance when necessary.

Physical prosperity includes maintaining a healthy way of life to diminish the risk of disease. Keeping up with physical wellness, for instance, can safeguard and foster the perseverance of an individual's breathing and heart function, strength, adaptability, and shape.

Caring for physical health and prosperity likewise implies diminishing the risk of a physical or health issue. For example:

- Limiting risks in the workplace
- Using contraception while engaging in sexual relations
- Basic hygiene
- Staying away from the use of tobacco, alcohol, or unlawful medications
- Getting the suggested immunizations for a particular condition or nation before traveling

Excellent physical health can pair with emotional wellness to develop an individual's general personal satisfaction.

- **Physical activity:** Most healthy children and adults ought to be consistently active, which should be a blend of both relaxing physical activity and an organized workout. Instances of everyday physical activity include climbing, trekking, and strolling. Instances of additional organized types of activity include strength-building weightlifting, running, and sports.
- **Nutrition and diet:** A balanced eating routine should contain starches, proteins, fats, vitamins, and minerals. Taking supplements should be done under the supervision of an authorized health professional. Liquid, preferably pure water, should be drunk routinely. Meals and snacks should be consumed throughout the day, and serving sizes should be sensible.

- **Alcohol and medications:** Substances that change mood or other cycles should be restricted or avoided. Those with habit-forming propensities or other health dangers should consider complete avoidance of these substances.
- **Medical taking care of oneself:** Basic things like daily prescription medication and over-the-counter pain relievers can be effectively dealt with at home. A professional should consider long-term coughing, fevers, or other kinds of sicknesses. When signs and side effects are noticeable or difficult, crisis treatment should be looked for.
- **Rest and sleep:** While regular activity is fundamental for physical health, permitting the body to rest is comparably significant. Investing energy in unwinding or lying down for brief rests can assist with reviving the body. Sleep should happen in a calm, dim climate and last roughly seven to nine hours. Reliable sleep that is a lot more limited or longer than this, or is of inferior quality, may be tended to by health professionals.

Let's move to a discussion of mental health. Are our physical health and mental health connected? Of course your mental health directly impacts your physical health, and countless studies and research conducted on how mental health affects physical health. If you want to be physically fit, you should also focus on your mental health.

The comprehensive meaning of mental health alludes to the prosperity of a person on deep social and mental levels. The condition of somebody's mental health has a critical influence over how they act, process feelings, and make decisions. An individual with excellent mental health can maintain healthy relationships, express a broad scope of feelings, and deal with the hardships of progress.

The World Health Organization (WHO) defines mental health as the kind of flourishing in which an individual understands their true capacity, deals with the typical anxieties of life, works gainfully and productively, and can contribute to their field.

Many people consider mental healthiness to be the lack of diagnosable problems. However, mental health is best approached as a continuum. Toward one side of the range are individuals who show dynamic strength and are equipped to accept life's vulnerabilities. People whose issues seriously affect day-to-day life are on the opposite side of the range. If somebody falls in the midpoint of the range, they probably think of their mental health as "fine."

It's conceivable, even expected, for individuals to fall somewhere in the center. Regardless of whether you have an analyzed condition and feel your work is okay in your everyday life, you might miss the mark on assets to adapt to an unexpected change. These are some of the signs that somebody's mental health is changing:

- Changes in sleeping and eating patterns
- Withdrawal from companions, family, and exercise.
- Loss of energy
- Increased moodiness and emotional episodes
- Inability to keep a normal schedule

In children and young adults, we frequently consider physical health over mental health considerably more. Guardians and caregivers put a lot of energy into guaranteeing kids grow up physically healthy, yet they might have a partial picture of physical health. Physical health has two focal parts.

1. Nutrition

Great nutrition is fundamental for everybody, but developing bodies need significantly more. A large group of vitamins and minerals is essential for physical health, as is the perfect proportions of protein and carbs. Adjusting your child's diet gives them a significantly improved opportunity to remain physically healthy.

2. Activity

It isn't easy to guarantee children get sufficient exercise and physical activity. With the multiplication of screens in everyday life, children and young adults are becoming more inactive. The Department of Health and Human Services (HHS) activity rules recommend that youth ages 6 to 17 get an hour or a greater amount of physical activity every day. Still, most children don't get anywhere close to that.

Television is probably the greatest offender of creating a stationary way of life. Children who watch at least three hours of TV each day are 65 percent more likely to become overweight than children who watch less than one hour daily. Screens of any kind adversely affect health, from sleep problems to learning trouble.

Physical health includes regular dental and vision checks to screen for advancement, and guarantee that children get sufficient rest to fuel their development. Your child's regular check-ups are the ideal chance to raise any inquiries you have regarding physical health and catch any issues creating problems from the beginning.

Although the mind and body are often viewed as separate, mental and physical health are closely related. Good mental health can positively affect your physical health. In return, poor mental health can negatively affect your physical health.

It's essential to have a positive attitude; some ways to do this include the following:

- **Finding a balance between negative and positive emotions.** Staying positive doesn't mean you don't feel negative emotions, like anger or sadness. You need to feel them so that you can move through difficult circumstances. They can help you to react to a problem. But you don't want those emotions to take over. For example, it's not helpful to keep thinking about bad things that happened in the past or worry about the future.

- **Attempting to hold onto positive emotions when you have them.** Enjoy some time off from negative information. Know when to quit perusing the news. Use social media to connect for help and feel associated with others; however, watch out. Try not to get drawn into certain stories and arguments, or compare your life with others.

- **Practicing appreciation** implies being grateful for the beneficial things in your life. It's useful to do this consistently by pondering what you are thankful for or recording it in a diary. These can be big things, such as help from friends and family, or easily overlooked details, like partaking in a great meal. It's useful to do this consistently by pondering what you are thankful for or recording it in a diary. Practicing appreciation can assist you with seeing your life in an unexpected way. For instance, when you are stressed, you may not see that there are other times when you have a few positive emotions. Appreciation can assist you with remembering them.

- **Dealing with your physical health**, since your physical and mental health is closely associated. **Being physically active.** Exercise can lessen feelings of stress and discouragement and work on your mindset.

- **Getting sufficient rest.** Rest influences your temperament. If you don't get decent rest, you might be all the more easily irritated and angry. Over the long term, an absence of quality rest can make you likely to become discouraged. So, it's essential to ensure that you have a rest plan and get sleep of sufficient quality consistently.

- **Healthy eating.** Great nutrition will assist you with feeling improved physically and may likewise work on your mindset and diminish uneasiness and stress. Insufficient specific nutrients might aggravate mental illnesses. For instance, there might be a connection between low levels of vitamin B12 and sadness. Eating a consistent diet can assist you with getting enough of the supplements you need.

- **Connecting with others**. Humans are social animals, and having solid, healthy relationships with others is essential. Having a social network might assist with safeguarding you against the damages of stress. Having various sorts of connections is likewise great. Other than connecting with loved ones, you could track down ways of engaging with your local area or neighborhood. For instance, you could join a neighborhood association or a group centered on a leisure activity you appreciate.
- **Encouraging a feeling of significance and reason in life.** This could be through your job, helping out, mastering new skills, or investigating your spirituality.
- **Creating adapting skills**, which are strategies you use to manage stressful circumstances. They can assist you with dealing with an issue, taking action, being adaptable, and not effectively surrendering in settling something.
- **Getting plenty of sunlight.** Drawing energy from the sun makes the brain release endorphins, hormones that support delight and diminish torment. Endorphins don't simply satisfy you; they can diminish emotional stress and advance a general feeling of prosperity. Sunlight is likewise an extraordinary wellspring of vitamin D. Besides delivering cerebral synthetics that can work on your state of mind, vitamin D can assist with mood. Low levels of vitamin D have been related to seasonal affective disorder (SAD), schizophrenia, and nervousness. So, take some time from your daily practice

and absorb energy from the sun. Most specialists agree that thirty minutes to two hours per day of sunlight can work on your mental health and, by and large, prosperity.

Spiritual health is a component of human well-being that coordinates all elements of health: physical, emotional, mental, and social. Spiritual health makes life meaningful and develops generosity, morals, and individual discernment.

Spiritual health is the glue that holds a wide range of various bits of health together. Spiritual health is different from other kinds of health because it is grounded in clinical exploration. Spirituality comes from the Latin word *spiritus*, signifying "breath" or "life." Different perspectives might bring about various spiritualities. For example, how Christians experience the supernatural varies significantly from how a Hindu sees the unity of all things being God.

One more degree of differentiation is the numerous denominations inside a religion. For example, how a Baptist Christian encounters God in Scripture profoundly differs from how a Catholic peruses Lectio Divina. Every order of a significant religion has specific approaches to communicating with the divine. Spirituality is a term that portrays a general way of connecting with the divine. Religion, in general, stresses the varying substance of the divine. Who for sure is the divine? The philosophy, regulations, or dharma varies, yet how one draws in the divine experientially is the "soul" or embodiment of the association. Jewish and Christian traditions have used scriptural words like *nephesh* (Hebrew) and *pneuma* (Greek) to hint at the possibility of completeness, breath, and the living standard. Eastern traditions like Hinduism, Buddhism, and Sikhism understand the significance of human breath and use it in their reflective practices. Early shamanic healing among Native Americans and Polynesians used comparable ceremonies of drawing and healing spiritual power inside one who needs it.

Spirituality is unity with sources of extraordinary power. Spirituality improves consciousness of God, further connection with love, hopeful openness towards the presence of God, and great meaningfulness. This prompts spiritual improvement. One can supplement spirituality with guidance and psychotherapy, influencing every part of individual development.

The spiritual component of health can be the most private piece of the puzzle while attempting to put every one of the eight elements of well-being together. For the most part, individuals like to carry on with life with meaning and reason. When these objectives are met, it produces agreement in one's life and the others they surround themselves with.

How might you work on your spiritual well-being? It's ideal to sort out what procedures work for you. Since spiritual health includes one's qualities, convictions, and reason, it tends to be accomplished in more ways than one, both physically and mentally.

1. Identify your spiritual focus. By investigating your spiritual center, you are basically asking yourself about the individual you are and your meaning. Ask yourself: Who am I? What is my motivation? What do I value most? These inquiries will lead you down a path where you will think more about yourself and permit yourself to see things about yourself that will assist you with satisfying self-realization.

2. Search for deeper meaning. Searching for deeper meaning in your life and dissecting patterns will assist you with seeing that you have command over your predetermination. Monitoring this can lead to a joyful and healthy life.

3. Get it out. Expressing what is on your mind will assist you with keeping an engaged mind. Following a monotonous day or a critical occasion, you might feel confused and need the option to sort out your feelings. By writing down your thoughts, you can think more clearly and push ahead.

4. Attempt yoga. Yoga is a physical strategy that can assist with working on your spiritual health by lessening emotional and physical stresses on your mind and body. Yoga is available at various levels and can assist with bringing down stress, supporting the skeletal system, lowering circulatory strain, and lessening tension, unhappiness, exhaustion, and sleeping disorders.

5. Travel. It's valid! Setting aside time for yourself to travel to a new location or a bright spot can give you time to think about your care. When you are where your mind can keep out interruptions and help you reflect and rest, you will have a superior association with yourself. This enables you to release tensions and concentrate intently on the best approach for general well-being. A few exercises to participate in when traveling include working out, talking with a guide or consultant, contemplation, or taking on a temporary commitment to silence.

6. Think positively. When you begin seeing things in your life in a positive way, you will wind up thinking differently and pulling together your mind to a bright, healthy spot. Likewise, you'll feel comforted when you wipe out pessimism and outline your thought process of specific things and circumstances in a more positive light.

7. Make time to meditate. While dealing with your time and everyday errands can be challenging, giving time to yourself is pivotal. Whether in the first part of the day when you awaken, during your midday break, or before bed, set aside five to ten minutes to meditate every day. Fitting this unwinding into your lifestyle will free your mind and encourage a more grounded relationship with your spiritual well-being.

Benefits Associated with Spirituality

One method for evaluating spirituality is to perceive that it assists individuals with understanding the meaning of life. Since spirituality consolidates different practices that are great for both body and mind, it can give individuals advantages to their mental health:

Works on confidence and control. People who practice spirituality can improve their levels of confidence, assurance, and tranquility within themselves. It helps an individual establish their identity, improves their connection with what they accept, and makes it easier for them to tolerate others regardless of their spiritual beliefs.

Fosters a feeling of community. People in a community with similar beliefs might find common ground via the shared experience of spirituality. Being a significant part of a coordinated religion has the potential to provide people with a rich means of social support. The community promotes social cooperation and dependability, both of which are beneficial to the mental health of individuals.

Encourages mindfulness. Spirituality is additionally connected with self-reflection and contemplation. These are healthy practices, and they impact an individual's mental state in a positive manner. Thus, one feels associated with others and has a meaningful existence. Besides, spiritual practices can inspire expression in forms like poetry, folklore, craftsmanship, and other disciplines.

Evolves unity with your environmental elements. Spiritually inclined people may seek out a sense of solidarity with their natural surroundings. Subsequently, people know about and value their physical climate. Moreover, spiritual lessons emphasize the importance of and serve as a foundation for making the best decisions. They exhibit forgiveness, appreciation, and empathy, all of which help people adjust to difficult situations.

Soothes a person's mind. Spirituality can assume a huge part in calming an individual's mind and giving one an uplifting outlook. Spirituality or religion can assist with diminishing stress and nervousness. An example would be how rigid rituals or practices can help outline design and consistency, which aids people going through trying circumstances. These exercises can help a person feel more at ease by enabling them to take a step back and adjust to stressful or nervous feelings.

CHAPTER 6

Embracing the Science of Complementary and Alternative Medicine

A healer's power stems not from any special ability, but from maintaining the courage and awareness to embody and express the universal healing power that every human being naturally possesses.

—Eric Micha'el Leventhal

Complementary medicine is a term used to depict the treatments you might use alongside traditional Western medicine. Instances of complementary medicine include massage, reflexology, biofeedback, yoga, reiki, music therapy, directed symbolism, and dietary enhancements.

Complementary and alternative medicine (CAM) is the term for clinical items and practices that are not a piece of standard clinical consideration. Individuals with disease may use CAM to help them cope with the symptoms of their illness, such as fatigue, pain, and sickness, as well as to comfort themselves and ease their condition about their illness and the stress that comes with it. They may feel that by using CAM, they are successfully taking care of themselves and working to treat or stop their malignant growth.

Integrative medicine is a way of dealing with clinical problems that combines traditional Western medicine with CAM approaches that have been shown to be safe and effective by scientific research. In many cases, this method lays therapeutic emphasis on the patient's tendencies and efforts to treat the psychological, physical, and spiritual aspects of their health.

Conventional medicine is a framework wherein health experts with an M.D. (medical doctor) or D.O. (doctor of osteopathy) degree treat side effects and illnesses using medications, radiation, or other medical procedures. It is likewise practiced by other health experts, like medical caretakers, drug specialists, doctor collaborators, and advisors. It might be called allopathic medicine, biomedicine, Western, standard, or conventional medicine. Some conventional clinical specialists are additionally experts in CAM.

Standard medicine has therapies that clinical specialists acknowledge as legitimate treatments for a particular kind of infection, and health-care experts broadly use it. Additionally, best practices, the standard of care, and the standard of therapy are maintained.

Complementary medicine is used alongside standard clinical treatment but isn't believed to be standard treatment without help from anyone else. One model uses needle therapy to assist with decreasing a few results of malignant growth treatment. Less examination has been done for most types of complementary medicine.

Elective medicine is used rather than standard clinical treatment. For example, one model uses a healthy diet to treat malignant growth rather than taking medication endorsed by an oncologist. Unfortunately, fewer studies have been completed for most kinds of elective medicine.

Each type of complementary medicine might focus on a particular part of your health. Complementary methodologies can give at least one of these health benefits:

- Ease pain
- Lessen anxiety and stress
- Lessen queasiness
- Increase relaxation
- Help heal injuries
- Encourage feelings of prosperity, delight, positivity, and inward peace
- Ease muscle strain
- Diminish tiredness
- Further develop flexibility and flow

What Are the Kinds of Complementary Therapies?

There are many kinds of complementary therapies. The following is a concise depiction of many of these methodologies.

Manipulation and Body-Based Practices

Massage. Massage seeks out your body's sensitive spots, and pressure focuses on advancing relaxation. There are many forms of massage, for instance shiatsu, Hellerwork, and reflexology. The most popular variety expands upon the five fundamental strokes of Swedish massage: effleurage (slow, cadenced skimming strokes to encourage blood flow towards the heart), petrissage (manipulating, squeezing, and moving muscle groups), grating (consistent pressure or tight round strokes, frequently used around joints), percussion (drumming hands on body), and vibration (rapid strokes shaking the muscle to and fro). Massage therapy has been used to decrease pressure and uneasiness, further develop the mindset, help in relaxation, and control pain. If you've had a medical procedure, massage can quicken healing of incisions and may forestall or diminish scarring. Foot massage has decidedly affected pain, sickness, and relaxation.

Reflexology. This therapy includes applying manual pressure to a region of your foot, hand, or ear that is accepted to correspond with the impacted organs or bones. Reflexology might assist with easing side effects like pain, obstruction, and sickness.

Chiropractic or osteopathic manipulation. This hands-on approach spotlights the spine and different joints of your body and their association with your sensory system. These methodologies include moving your muscles and joints using extension, delicate pressure, and obstruction. They can assist with facilitating muscle torment and work on your general portability and capacity. This approach can assist with diminishing the seriousness of different side effects, including headaches, PMS, and carpal passage condition.

Measuring. This kind of massage therapy includes using warmed cups to make a vacuum on your skin, and it increases the blood flow to designated regions to lessen the irritation.

Mind-Body Techniques

Meditation. Meditation is a technique for relaxing and calming your mind to ease muscle strain and gain internal harmony. There are various forms of meditation, taught exclusively or in social scenes.

Relaxation and deep breathing. Relaxation and breathing techniques help deliver muscle pressure, ease breathing, decrease uneasiness, and empower a special feeling of control, especially while taking unpleasant medicines.

Yoga. Yoga is a mild exercise comprising body stances and breathing techniques, and it has been practiced for thousands of years in India and is presently famous all over the planet. In the West, yoga is esteemed more for its physical than mental advantages; for example, its capacity to increase gracefulness and authority and ease pressure and weakness.

Landscape therapy. Landscape therapy is the appearance of quiet, relaxing landscapes that can inspire serenity. Landscapes might be displayed in an obscured room through a slide-show or video screen, or they might be displayed as craft books or artwork. Landscape therapy is often used as an interruption procedure to assist with overseeing pain and uneasiness.

Music therapy. Music therapy is a fine expressive art intended to assist people with accomplishing concordance and equilibrium. Music therapy can include both listening to and/ or playing music. Music specialists are experts who plan music programs for patients. Through music, you explore mental and behavioral issues close to home. Music therapy can assist with processing feelings and advancing relaxation. Listening to music can be either calming or invigorating.

Animal-assisted therapy. A specialist collaborates with dogs or other animals to assist you with better adapting to your medical problems, including psychological disorders, cancer, and heart disease. Animal-assisted therapy can diminish pain, uneasiness, despair, and weakness related to numerous medical conditions.

Biofeedback. This is a method through which you figure out how to control your thoughts, feelings, and behavior. Your specialist will quantify your body's capacities (for instance, EEG to gauge brain waves, ECG to gauge heart rate, EMG to quantify muscle contractions) through therapy, and you'll see changes in these estimations as you learn new coping methods.

Directed symbolism or representation. With this therapy, a specialist assists you with making positive mental pictures and wanted results for exact circumstances. For instance, while in a condition of relaxation, you could zero in on feeling more grounded or better, or picture the obliteration of tumor cells. In another method, you might imagine different parts of treatment, from the most innocuous to the most agonizing, keeping quiet and relaxed at each progression.

Hypnotherapy. Hypnotherapy is like directed symbolism, yet a doctor or authorized subliminal specialist prompts profound relaxation.

Prayer therapy. This approach uses prayer restoratively for mental and close-to-home recuperating. Prayer can be used to explore your heart's/soul's past, present, or future pain and stress. This can assist you with bettering your understanding of yourself and exploring and processing feelings. Your prayer is private—the specialist just goes about as a facilitator.

Energy Force Therapies

Kendo. Kendo is a noncombative martial art that uses breathing techniques, and groupings of slow, elegant developments to work on the progression of qi, or "life energy," to quiet the mind and advance self-healing. It is frequently depicted as "meditation moving." It is presented more as a form of preventive medical care than as a reaction to an illness.

Qi gong. Qi gong is an ancient arrangement of development, breathing techniques and meditation. It's intended to create and work on the flow of qi, or "life energy," around your body.

Therapeutic touch. With therapeutic touch, a professional synchronizes their energy field with yours so disruptions in the "energy stream" are adjusted, and your body's healing powers can work freely. The specialist's hands range over your body and carefully evaluate any progressions or blockages in the energy field. Healing energy is guided from the specialist's body to yours. Touch therapy is used to treat pressure-related conditions like exhaustion and migraines and help with discomfort, particularly from muscle strain and following a medical procedure. It has additionally been used to advance injury healing and for lymphatic and flow disorders.

Reiki. Reiki is a form of Japanese spiritual healing that has its foundations in ancient Tibetan Buddhism. Reiki attempts to advance well-being, keep up with prosperity, and assist you with achieving a more elevated level of self-knowledge. Professionals direct "reiki energy" through their hands (holding them over your dressed body), diverting energy to areas of need in you. Reiki professes to adjust the body's energy points or "chakras" and disintegrate energy blockages that lead to disharmony and disease. Certain individuals might feel relaxed after treatment; others feel invigorated.

Acupuncture. Acupuncture is an ancient Chinese arrangement of medical care. It plans to forestall and fix explicit diseases and conditions by sticking extremely fine, strong needles into points of your body. Needle therapy is accepted to energize endorphins—natural pain relievers—which can likewise build sensations of prosperity. Acupressure, in which the equivalent acupoints are stimulated through pressure, might also be effective but less powerful.

Magnets. This therapy includes putting magnets on your body to lessen pain or improve healing.

Expressive Therapies

Journal writing. Writing in a journal is a powerful method for handling some of the feelings that living with an ailment trigger.

Communicating your sentiments to others can be troublesome if you're confronting a significant disease. However, journal writing can securely and secretly communicate troublesome sentiments. Customary journal writing may likewise assist you with explaining your considerations and using sound judgment.

Art therapy. Drawing, painting, and sculpting, particularly in a group setting, can assist you with communicating sentiments that can't be quickly expressed.

Support groups. In support gatherings, you have the opportunity to share your interests, fears, and expectations with people who are encountering similar life challenges. Support groups can help your loved ones as well.

Other Complementary Methodologies

Dietary enhancements and natural cures. Dietary enhancements include vitamins, minerals, hormones, and catalysts that aren't overseen by the U.S. Food and Drug Administration for security and adequacy. Examples include glucosamine, chondroitin, St. John's Wort, ginkgo, saw palmetto, ginseng, fish oil, echinacea, vitamin D, garlic calcium, and green tea.

Aromatherapy. In aromatherapy, you're presented with essential oils. The oils might be vaporized in a room or absorbed through your skin. The aromas delivered by the oil are thought to follow up on your nerve center, the part of the mind that impacts your hormones. In theory, a smell could influence your temperament, digestion, anxiety, and sex drive. Some essential oils include chamomile, lavender, peppermint, rosemary, eucalyptus, sandalwood, and tea tree. Decisions and reactions to fragrances are profoundly private.

Risks of Complementary and Alternative Medicines

Many individuals think complementary therapies are more secure than regular clinical medicines since they are more natural. This isn't correct all of the time. There are various well-being and legal issues encompassing the utilization of complementary therapies that you should know about.

Complementary therapies are used along with traditional clinical medicines to assist with working on an individual's health and prosperity. Models include needle therapy, aromatherapy, traditional Chinese medication, homegrown medication, yoga, meditation, and massage. These medicines are sometimes referred to as a group as complementary and elective medication (CAM).

Estimates propose that the number of Australians who use complementary medicines or talk with complementary advisors is on the ascent. Nonetheless, there are numerous well-being and legitimate issues encompassing their utilization.

Therapeutic Products That Contain Certain Vitamins or Minerals

- Nutritional supplements
- Homeopathic medicines
- Certain aromatherapy products

- Traditional medicines such as Chinese, ayurvedic, and Australian Indigenous

Clinical trials are important. We are unable to know for certain if a complementary therapy is effective without first doing preliminary clinical research. Both the immediate and the long-term risks associated with the therapy are currently unknown. An absence of logical proof shouldn't imply that a complementary therapy doesn't work. It might mean that the current research is not available or that the accessible information doesn't satisfy guidelines for clinical preliminaries.

If you are interested in starting complementary medicine, here are some tips:

- Talk with your primary health-care provider before starting any complementary medication or treatment.
- Ask your health-care provider for their suggestion for a complementary practitioner. You can likewise explore nearby medical clinic sites.
- Look for professional organizations for the sort of specialist you need. For instance, if you're interested in a chiropractor, look for chiropractor organizations in your area. You can learn about the requirements for licensing or necessary certifications and typically find links to professionals in your area.
- Do as much research as possible on the individual specialist you are thinking about visiting, including looking into their education, training, licenses, or certificates. You may get this information by looking

on their website, or you can phone their office and ask for it before scheduling an appointment.

- See whether the complementary professional will work with your primary health-care provider. It is essential to ensure that all of your providers collaborate with one another in order to provide you with the best possible care.
- Inquire as to whether they've worked with people with your particular health condition(s).
- Check with your health insurance company to see whether or not supplemental treatments will be covered, as well as what personal charges you should plan for.
- Maintain a record of all your current health-care providers, as well as your regular and complementary medicine specialists, in addition to the most up-to-date information about the totality of your prescribed medications and any other health products or treatments you make use of. This will provide all of the professionals involved a comprehensive understanding of the steps you take to address your health concerns.
- See your current health-care provider if your side effects continue or worsen.

How to determine whether a complementary therapy is safe, effective, and backed by science? It's important to keep in mind that clinical research evidence for the safety and effectiveness of complementary therapy may not be available for all methods. If you want to learn more about specific methodologies, you can take the following steps:

- Talk with your current health-care provider. Inform them about the complementary therapies you're thinking about. Request their opinion of the safety and efficacy of these methodologies.

- Ask the complementary provider for evidence that their methods are safe and effective for your health condition.
- Visit or call your local library or a medical library (clinical schools and some medical clinics have them). Ask for help finding articles or books that make sense about the complementary therapy or product you're interested in.
- Visit trustworthy sites. The U.S. government has a few organizations that give supportive information. These include the National Center for Complementary and Integrative Health, the U.S. Food and Drug Administration, and the National Institutes of Health Office of Dietary Supplements.

CHAPTER 7

Reading

There are books in every part of the world. College campuses, institutions in general, and larger metropolitan cities all have an abundance of bookshops and libraries of all sizes and designs. They are completely loaded up with one of the most important inventions ever—books. People who read books value the fact that they may be obtained in such a wide variety of settings. Those who don't have a strong reading habit themselves can't possibly comprehend what it is that makes certain people so obsessed with reading. Nevertheless, there is a rationale that supports the preoccupation they have. You are continually encouraged to read on a regular basis.

Reading might seem to be nothing more than simple frivolity to certain people. It's possible, though, that it's helping both your mind and body, even if you're not conscious that it's doing so. Reading can therefore be more significant than simply learning knowledge. For individuals who hate reading, you might alter your perspective in the wake of finding out about the advantages. Reading can be an extraordinary advantage to you in various ways, such as sharpening your brain, creative mind, and composing abilities. When there are so many advantages to reading, it seems like it should be an everyday occurrence to read something extraordinary.

Importance of Reading Books

Reading is crucial because it develops our reasoning, provides us with lasting knowledge and examples, and keeps our minds active. In contrast to other things in our world, books have the unique capacity to store and maintain a diverse variety of information as well as stories, sentiments and ideas. The significance of a book to help us learn and comprehend things can't be overstated.

Is it possible for words, chapters, and made-up worlds to have a significant positive impact on one's health? They very definitely can, because reading is a timeless form of both entertainment and information.

As a matter of fact, reading was the main source of personal entertainment for a very considerable period of time, and it's possible that this is why reading has been at the center of attention for so long. Reading has persisted over the years, and thankfully, the benefits of reading have also endured along with the books themselves. So, we should discuss a few reasons why reading is so important.

The advantages of reading range from improving emotional and physical well-being to providing you with knowledge to make more informed decisions. It's not a big surprise that books and reading are at the top of the most popular pastimes.

Although books have been around for what seems like eternity, they have not lost their significance. The following is a list of some of the incredible benefits that come from getting a decent book and immersing yourself in words.

Benefits of Reading Books

1. Cognitive Mental Stimulation and Brain Exercise

Reading is an extraordinary pastime for some individuals. However, it also provides various benefits for your mental health in the form of increased thinking and comprehension. Focusing on the words and the storyline invigorates your brain and cognitive capacities. This particular sensation may help to sharpen your thinking, specifically the portion of your brain that is responsible for focus and basic analysis. Reading works on this region of the brain in a manner similar to how sharpening a blade does. Because of this strengthening of the brain, your attention will eventually be elevated when you are concentrating on anything significant.

And how does reading sharpen your mind? It does so through stimulation of the brain. By making you focus strongly on the words, your brain takes in a lot of information, which stimulates your critical thinking and analysis skills. This stimulation is good for your mind and sharpens your point of view. Isn't it astounding how a book can do that? The finest people on the planet read regularly and are aware of how essential knowledge is. So, it can be an ideal opportunity to consider their advice to get nearer to your dream.

Reading doesn't simply assist your critical thinking; it further develops your brain power. Consider what happens when you work a muscle consistently. That muscle develops and turns out to be more flexible than it was before. Your mind operates similarly when you read. Reading regularly stimulates the brain in a way similar to how working out stimulates a muscle; it enhances the many parts of the brain that control your thinking and analytical skills.

2. Vocabulary and Knowledge Expansion

While reading, you might come across a few words you don't quite understand or even recognize. As a result, you may decide to look up the word and learn its meaning. Word references in the book's structure may help you learn a new word that you might not understand. The act of searching for the meaning helps your brain resist recalling the previously unknown term, since you had no idea what it meant to begin with. Think just how much your vocabulary has grown since you first learned how to read. You now know many new words that are more clever sounding than when you initially began reading.

How does this help you? Indeed, after a few days of reading and researching unfamiliar terms, your vocabulary will begin to grow, one word at a time. When you read on a regular basis, new words and expressions enter your brain, providing you with another vocabulary that you could never have acquired otherwise. This is demonstrated in a study by the University of Oregon.

You probably won't understand how much your vocabulary has expanded after only one day of heavy reading. However, you will start to incorporate these words you have been learning into your everyday vocabulary, and you will begin to discover yourself using them. The amount you take in while reading is unimaginable, and this part of understanding is one more critical advantage of daily reading.

3. Stress and Tension Relief

An overwhelming majority of people are aware of the fact that reading is an excellent kind of entertainment; nevertheless, you and the others probably won't be aware of the fact that reading may aid with bringing down stress levels. Though true, nonetheless it sounds strange when spoken out loud. Reading and focusing on the written word might help you to clear your thoughts of stress and day-to-day worries. By taking your mind off the tensions of everyday life, you can relax and allow the stress to melt away.

It's hard to believe, but reading may help relieve stress in surprising ways. When you read a book, your brain instantly transports itself to another world where it encounters a variety of different individuals. Someone who is frazzled or who goes through extended periods of stress may find that this change in pace provides a much-needed sense of relief and revitalization. By reading, you can permit yourself to slowly inhale, unwind, and be transported to a different place or time through the words composed on the page.

Stress can influence many pieces of your daily life, and after long periods of extended stress, it might be hurtful to your overall well-being. Reading books and other writings can assist with addressing the issues that stress causes by permitting your mind and body to unwind. When you begin reading, you focus not on your stress but the words and storyline. Reading will bring down your stress level, encouraging you mentally and physically.

4. Depression and Dysthymia Assistance

Reading, particularly self-improvement guides, can assist with warding off depressive episodes. Like bringing down your stress levels, reading animates the piece of the brain that is associated with depression too. Self-improvement guides, loaded with information about how to better yourself and your perspective, can assist with lessening depression. People who suffer the negative impacts of troublesome thoughts but not to the extent that they need medicine may find that reading books is quite beneficial.

You may discover manuals to self-improvement at any physical or online bookshop. Despite this, they are not the only books that have been shown to lessen the severity of certain people's depressive episodes. Novels, short stories, magazine articles, and even true-life books may all contribute, in their own ways, to the process of lowering these tendencies. Reading allows you to shift your attention away from the factors that are contributing to your melancholy and toward those that may provide you with new perspectives. Because of this, you will not in general feel worried about the onerous situation you are in. All things being equal, you are focused on the story.

Treating depression can appear to be an odd advantage of reading. However, the stimulation of the brain is incredibly useful in regard to facilitating recovery from depression. The feeling of joy that likewise comes from reading can light up your state of mind, helping your day transform from depression to happiness. Obviously, reading is certainly not a super-durable fix for a major issue, yet it can assist with diminishing the troubles of depression. Reading works similarly to how a painkiller eases joint discomfort.

5. Memory Improvement and Better Focus

Additionally, while it has been referenced before that reading can further develop focus and critical thinking, there is one more component of psychological well-being that reading supports with getting to the next level. NCU expresses this point on their blog: reading, even just a little bit every day, may help you improve both your capacity to focus and your memory. Reading animates the brain in this occurrence, especially the piece of the brain that assists with memory and thought. Like physical activity, reading is a mental activity that stretches your memory and focuses on the edges.

Reading comprehension at the most fundamental level strengthens your memory skills. Remember the assessments you took in elementary school where you had to estimate how much information you had retained while reading brief stories? Indeed, reading perception as a grown-up works the same way. While reading, your brain continually holds snippets of information about the story. Since the piece of the brain that controls memory is animated, this behaves like an exercise for this piece of the brain, bringing about superior memory.

How is your focus affected by reading? Reading improves your ability to focus, since it trains your brain to anticipate having to better understand the material. While plunking down to read a book or article, you won't comprehend what you are reading unless you're focused. Consider what it is like while solving a numerical equation. To get it right, you need to focus entirely on that problem. The equivalent goes for reading. Your capacity to concentrate is strengthened, which helps with improving your general ability to focus. This is similar to the way your brain works with memory.

6. Writing Ability Strengthening

Reading doesn't only have health benefits; reading also has benefits for other parts of your life. These benefits help to make readers balanced people. Individuals who write know the significance of reading. Whether you write things for work or for fun, reading can further develop your writing abilities and capacities. Reading may improve your writing skills in a variety of different ways, many of which take place without you even being aware of it. Reading is one of the most effective methods to improve your writing skills.

Writers are often avid readers too, in light of the fact that they look for the satisfaction of reading. By focusing on how books and stories are set up and composed, you can mirror these styles, consequently further developing your writing abilities significantly. Concentrating on the writing of others is an incredible tool, particularly if you appreciate the writing. Indeed, even top-rated writers use this tool for concentrating on writing styles and subjects.

The most amazing aspect of reading about the evolution of writing is that there are multiple volumes that concentrate on improving your writing. You can find these self-improvement guides online or at any bookstore. If you consider yourself a noteworthy essayist, you may want to read these remarkable books on writing, although reading in any form may be a big contributor to the improvement of your writing.

7. Imagination and Empathy Improvement

Although improving your imagination isn't one of the more normal advantages, reading can expand your imagination. Consider the worlds you are submerged in and the characters you encounter while reading a book. The part of your brain that controls imagination gets animated as a result of these dimensions and characters, causing you to picture what the places and people seem like just by imagining the words.

When you start reading a book, you generally don't have an image in your mind toward the beginning. Nonetheless, when completing the book, you can undoubtedly envision the whole world and characters that fill the book. Reading books stimulates the brain. Avid readers will know the feeling of losing themselves in the realms of books. It is a great feeling.

Imagination is an incredible asset that can be valuable in all parts of life. Though it probably isn't thought about in this way very often, the imagination permits us to be sympathetic to individuals. This empathy can help at work or even at home. With reading being a great method for working on your imagination, it's no big surprise books have been the number 1 form of entertainment for countless years.

8. Sleep Boost

Did you have any idea that reading can likewise assist with your rest? No, this doesn't imply that reading assists you with nodding off. Instead, it contributes to further building your overall pattern of relaxation and the calming qualities you possess. Reading, since it empowers you to unwind and de-stress, can assist with transitioning you into a profound and serene rest. It may sound too good to be true, yet reading can, as a matter of fact, assist you with resting.

Reading a book is a great activity to include in your nighttime routine just before you go to sleep. Selecting a good book and then settling in for the evening is remarkably relaxing. If your day is busy, calmly inhale. You can help yourself relax and calm down before falling asleep by setting aside specific times for reading just before bedtime. Of course, the sort of literature you read is your preference. Simply reading is the important part.

Reading before bed calms your body and mind, particularly following a long and stressful day. Regardless of whether the reading is only a short section or two, the quiet that reading instigates can assist with slipping you into a profound and soothing rest. The relaxation that books can bring is only one of the great advantages of reading consistently before bed.

9. Partake in Your Entertainment and Peace

Maybe the most notable advantage of reading is the entertainment benefit of opening a book with fresh, white pages. Naturally, the enjoyment of reading constantly inspires eager readers to acquire the next fantastic book. Reading has long been seen as a strong type of entertainment. Simply stated, reading is ideal for entertaining. Yet, there's something else to reading besides the entertainment factor.

Readers realize that reading can be quiet and promote relaxation. You can feel any stress or worry dissolve away by drenching yourself in a decent book. You are entertained and relaxed by simply reading, which is just one of the many wonderful features of books.

With the capacity to amuse as well as promote calmness, reading has been a consistent solace to individuals of any age and from varying backgrounds. For a long time, this entertainment factor has been at the forefront of literature. Books and other types of creative writing are still just as famous today as when they were invented. But lately, reading has been just as amazing for relaxation as it has been for enjoyment. Many outstanding readers and scholars have referenced the significance of reading throughout their professions, being advocates for reading.

10. Reading Can Brighten Your Day

Books consistently can welcome happiness into your life. Reading not only has significant positive effects on one's mental and physical health, but it also has the power to brighten one's day. Sometimes the days might be difficult and troublesome, but reading provides that release at the end of the day to lessen and replace the burden with cheer. There isn't a compelling justification for having a negative view under difficult situations. Simply take a break from your day, read for a short while, and feel yourself unwinding. Even though mindfulness and yoga may be effective at uplifting your day, spending a short time alone with a book is a guaranteed great way to get through your evening or night. Books are not difficult to carry around, especially with the easy access made possible with tablets and technology. You can partake in reading time anywhere.

Reading is a good way to relax in a bustling world, whether it's on vacation or just for a few moments while waiting in the carpool line. If you are an early riser, it's a good idea to begin your day with a little light reading. You can breathe easily, and your day might be a little bit more brilliant. Take a few seconds for yourself and allow books to drop a little weight from your shoulders so you can partake in the things around you.

11. Reading Broadens Your Mind

Books help you understand things according to a broader point of view. Reading a book about a specific culture, for instance, can assist you with understanding how that culture varies from your own. Regardless of whether you agree with another culture's opinions, you learn the knowledge and facts necessary to expand your understanding and perspective.

Books give you new ideas. While reading, you continually discover new things, and you can start to view the world from a more balanced viewpoint. Without different perspectives, one will generally have a one-layered kind of thinking based on their lifetime experiences.

We behave in the way that we do based on what we learned in our formative years. We check out things from the viewpoint of our insight. Using this as a point of focus, it is simple to assume that our method is the correct one. Books can help us reconsider ideas, letting go of right and wrong concepts and allowing us to see a variety of human perspectives.

For instance, consider a picture of a Muslim woman wearing a burka or hijab. Many individuals in Western culture might see this as a sort of mistreatment. But truly, numerous Muslim women decide to dress like this as an expression of their deep-seated beliefs.

If you were to read a book or article about this issue composed by a Muslim woman, you would begin seeing things according to her point of view. It's a huge world out there, and reading is one method for expanding your mind to all of the many possibilities that exist.

Books are amazing things that can be entertaining and beneficial to your health. They are practical tools for a healthy lifestyle. Individuals who don't read can't figure out the adoration for reading. However, people who read consistently know the significance of immersing themselves in a great book. The books you decide to read are your preference, which can go from emotional to factual. Frequently, individuals will read magazine articles or even textbooks assuming that is what they like. No matter what you decide to read, you can depend on the different advantages of reading to help both your mind and body.

CHAPTER 8

Helping Others Learn and Grow

When you consider what you've learned, the first thing that likely comes to mind is probably something you were taught at school—for instance, the French words you need to be familiar with for an upcoming test. Learning such things could be beneficial in the future should you at some point visit France.

Learning information (like French vocabulary) can be very significant. However, in addition to learning from books, you can also learn from and about those around you. This process of picking up new information while interacting with others is known as social pick-up. Models are learned from or about others since, for this sort of learning, people are the source. More often than not, you are surrounded by others, including your family, educators, and school friends. In this way, you can benefit from and learn about others, perhaps without even realizing it!

Since humans are such social beings, social learning is an important ability. Social learning is an extremely proficient method for learning things. For instance, you don't need to figure everything out on your own since you can learn from the mistakes and successes of others. Likewise, social learning can empower you to realize others better and understand how to behave around them more readily. These kinds of social skills help you build strong relationships with other people, which is highly beneficial for your prosperity.

Coaching is an interaction. It is helping other people learn, develop, and push toward their desires or new experiences throughout everyday life and work. The interaction consists of a variety of specific actions, such as tuning in. Coaching is more than that, or as we like to say today, a mentality.

A coaching mentality might be seen as a caring attitude to some extent. We move beyond our plan for the other person. We don't attempt to fix them or inspire them to adjust to our picture of what they ought to be, do, feel, or think. In our examination, we call this approach coaching with empathy. We balance that with what many people frequently do, in an attempt to fix, right, or assist somebody with adjusting to what we figure they ought to do. We call this coaching for consistency.

This requires humility and caring for the other person. It sounds straightforward, in light of the fact that it is so essentially human. In any case, given the day-to-day burdens around us, this turns into a significant accomplishment. While confronting such tensions, it is challenging to put the requirements and wants of others over our own.

How can we maintain a meaningful and romantic existence?

This is a profound inquiry. Since philosophers, strong leaders, and other perceptive individuals have fought to respond for literally millennia, it is an inquiry we should likely debate on a more regular basis.

One of the big guarantees of approachable leadership is that agreeability doesn't simply impact your authority. It further develops associations in all aspects of your life. You can now add to that list by saying that assisting others provides your life a sense of meaning and purpose.

Consider your own life. Have you at any point been miserable? Perhaps you were battling with a family partner or a companion. Perhaps you felt overpowered or that you were wasting your time. Perhaps you felt lost and overlooked. How engrossed would you describe your use of your workaround at the time? Is it accurate to say that you were eager to attend, or were things just about to end?

It happens to us all. We're human. However much we attempt to keep all that in its own compartment, it's unimaginable. Everyday events have an impact on all the others. Think about the person who most influenced your development into who you are.

Or, on the other hand, consider a few people. Think back to a single moment when you realized, discovered, or learned something that has stuck with you, possibly up until this moment. At that time, what did the other person say or do? How did they cause you to feel?

We have affected countless people all over the planet in this reflection. They most commonly convey to us that the individual frequently considered them, listened to them, inspired them, and put them to the test. It wasn't often that the focus of the situation was them fitting into the workplace culture or completing a task. Nor was it applied to work-related performance. All things being equal, it was a more profound thing. And in many situations, the impact is felt years after the occurrence.

When you learn about others, you realize what they resemble and how they act. For this type of learning, it's important to concentrate on other people's behaviors so you can use this knowledge to guide future decisions.

For instance, envision telling one of your colleagues that you like the person sitting two tables away. However, you quickly discover that your coworker is incredibly unreliable when your secret ends up being revealed to the entire office. Naturally you are extremely disturbed! In this situation, you might have learned that it is best not to share your personal feelings to her.

Although there are many things you can find out about others, numerous researchers concentrate on how we find out about others' trustworthiness. Knowing who to trust is essential because it enables you to decide whether you can believe what someone says.

Researchers have found that during our younger years, we become better and quicker at realizing who we can and cannot trust. In addition, we become better at finding out about others during our own development along these lines. As a result, social growth teaches us how to conduct ourselves in the company of other people, which is an essential skill for developing meaningful relationships.

Rousing characteristics normally relate to subjects of self-awareness, self-esteem, and self-discipline. But be that as it may, a person can be empowered by anyone who imitates the qualities they are longing for themselves.

More effective leaders are those that frequently influence those around them. They can serve as examples of how to use creativity to overcome obstacles, adapt under pressure, and engage with your resources.

1. Be the one to listen. We experience a daily reality that is clamoring to be heard. Lots of people are talking between virtual entertainment, websites, video diaries, webcasts, and conventional media, yet relatively few are listening As a result, when you put in the extra effort to listen, whether it be to your children, your neighbor, or that person in the grocery store, you are teaching two things: that the person speaking has value, and that you are interested in helping them grow. The better your listening abilities, the more others will search you out for that purpose. And frequently, people will find their way to development without your maxim.

2. Be the first one to laugh. Comic piano player Victor Borge once said, "Laughter is the shortest distance between two people." Nothing helps a person more than being able to share a laugh during stress, difficult situations, or times of delight. That is because laughter creates positivity. And positivity is fundamental for anybody attempting to develop. Personal development frequently accompanies mistakes, bumps, and bruises, so it's particularly helpful when we have somebody to help us laugh our way through the difficult times.

3. Rush to encourage. Consider this compelling story about a lady who died following a long-term fight with an uncommon type of disease. Many people stood at the lady's funeral and shared stories about how she had always been ready to listen, quick to laugh, and eager to pay attention to those around her.

After the service, as her family received guests, one guest drew nearer and said, "I believe you should know how this woman affected me. She never neglected to let me know I had a good heart whenever I saw her. She simply said, 'You have a good heart.' She's the only person who, at any point, was truthful to me about who I truly am. For that, I'm thankful."

Now and again, we neglect to encourage others. It's not because we can't see good in them; for the most part, it's simply that we don't think to refer to it. In any event, it's crucial that we frequently notice good qualities in others that they are unable to recognize in themselves. They may already have these insights, but having someone else mention them in a genuine manner makes a difference in ways we can't even imagine. When someone else recognizes and affirms the truth about who someone is capable of being, it goes a long way toward empowering them to realize their potential.

Helping people grow benefits them on a personal and professional level.

Great leaders contemplate growing their business. We cultivate long-term perspectives, evaluate our strengths and weaknesses, and set specific goals. Unfortunately, numerous business owners neglect to put a similar spotlight on helping employees grow.

Too often, employers fail to distinguish between what the business requires of its employees and what the employees need to accomplish their goals. Because they lack the proper insight, they don't provide the support and proper environment to help their employees succeed.

Stage 1: Recognize that change is hard, and give it focus and responsibility.

Change is, in every case, hard; for instance, 80 percent of New Year's goals are abandoned by mid-February. That is why worker growth—which is about change—frequently takes secondary place to other business concerns. The key to successful development is to assist the necessary changes with the same planning, diligence, and responsibility you would use for any other significant business goal.

An extraordinary method to identify needs is having an open discussion with your employees about their professional ambitions. For certain employees, it may very well be to bring in more cash to help their families; others might want to become a CEO. Having this discussion is a great way to demonstrate your responsibility for the well-being of your employees.

Stage 2: Look for collaborations between business requirements and representative ambitions.

When you understand your employees' professional ambitions, search for objectives within the company and ways that you could create mutual benefits. For instance, a line laborer who needs to support his family more readily could do so by ascending to an administrative level. On the other hand, a worker with aspirations of becoming CEO could develop skills by advancing to increasingly challenging responsibilities. In both cases, there's a collaboration with the business needs because the representative's growth implies that they likewise become more important to the company.

You can discover that an employee's long-term goals conflict with what the company needs. These discussions are important.

Stage 3: Set specific goals.

After recognizing the group's needs, set specific development goals for growth. Next, recognize specific assignments the employee can achieve to push toward their goals to satisfy company needs. For example, an employee who aspires to be promoted to line manager can prepare for their upcoming responsibilities by covering for an outgoing boss. Taking on extra endeavors may be the goal for an employee who aspires to become CEO in order to increase their openness and knowledge.

Stage 4: Agree on an action plan.

For every objective, settle on a course of action with defined dates. For instance, you could concur that the line employee will take a class in administrative abilities toward the second quarter's end. With the prospective CEO, you could distinguish the specific endeavors they will take on and when they will present them. The action plan should be reasonable. However, it should be specific enough so both you and the employee know what should be finished to accomplish the objective. It likewise ought to include a few important achievements for the next development.

It's likewise important to settle on how you will gauge the employee's progress in accomplishing the objective. Distinguish what specific results will be apparent to both you and the employee, telling you that the person in question has accomplished the objective.

Stage 5: Commit to natural progress and feedback.

Follow-up and feedback are the most important aspects of professional development. Therefore, you should make a commitment to reporting on your development goals at scheduled intervals. For instance, if you have routine status meetings with your employees, you could devote a certain amount of time once per month to recording your progress on development goals. The goal is to ensure you and the employee keep up with the focus on their development, resolve any issues that might emerge, and provide the employee the feedback that's vital for progress.

When it is done well, development planning can be a very rewarding experience for the employee, the supervisor, and the employer. Various organizations have their own thoughts and standards of what leadership material resembles in their company culture, and those qualities aren't generally self-evident or transparently imparted to most workers searching for progression. However, there are a few tried-and-true techniques that, when successfully applied, can give you the upper hand over less qualified peers and place you on a short list for promotion.

1. Center around making others successful.

Successful leaders ensure they have the perfect individuals working for them—the right skills, the proper disposition, a drive to succeed—and afterward motivate them to do incredible things. Leadership isn't about you. However, helping others become successful and eliminating the snags—over-the-top administration, personal conflict, vulnerability, and negative ideologies—help that achievement.

The key focus of leaders at all levels must be getting to know people and understanding what resources and conditions they require to perform at their best. One factor that is particularly important is providing individuals with sufficient independence to exercise some control over aspects of their current circumstance as well as the actual work itself. This can include anything from the way in which their office space is organized to the methods by which desired results are achieved. The perception of independence can be the difference between a labor force that is attracted and one that is merely conditional, exchanging time and effort for money.

2. Convey a powerful vision.

For individuals to genuinely focus on an objective, they need to know the "why" of the work. They have to understand that their efforts are making a difference and that there is a greater purpose to what is transpiring as a result of their spending a significant portion of their waking hours on it.

Extraordinary leaders communicate that purpose in the form of a compelling vision—a positive future state or accomplishment for which everyone must play an important role. For this, leaders should dominate vital narrating—the capacity to make, in basic and comprehensive language, motivational pictures that draw out the feelings, tap into individuals' qualities and dreams, and connect their persistent effort and everyday exercises to a more promising future they helped make.

3. Convey positive outcome.

Leaders who fail to produce important outcomes are rarely in charge for very long. To be seen as a good leader, you need to have traits like decisiveness, diligence, and achievement in constantly changing settings and environments, where you may have needed to get things done through other people.

New leaders can improve their ability to get things done by looking for opportunities that let them make important decisions and lead people toward a common goal. For example, joining a charitable board or the leadership council of a neighborhood group, or choosing to lead a major new project at work, can present opportunities and sharpen the skills needed to consider the options, listen to instinct, and make the hard decisions that lead to important results.

4. Create associations using key networking.

It's not exactly possible for leaders who want to affect change to remain undetected. To lead is to exert influence over a large number of partners both inside and outside of an association, as well as to earn their acceptance and support for change initiatives and innovative ideas. Shrewd leaders achieve their goals by creating areas of strength for partners and allies, looking past their nearby circle of influence.

They distinguish key partners and power players who can influence others for their sake. They endeavor to find natural connections with amazing outsiders who can give creative solutions and meaningful feedback on complex issues and connect them to basic assets that benefit the association.

These leaders don't let psychological tendencies like self-preoccupation or a lack of relational expertise prevent them from building relationships and expanding their organizations. Finally, they build established connections based on the interests of others, demonstrating that they are providers first rather than merely clients who are only interested in taking.

5. Increase mindfulness and self-observing.

Leaders' interactions and behavioral patterns are being closely scrutinized due to increased perceptibility and a higher standard. Words have more weight and might be misinterpreted. Messages are analyzed for any signs of suggestion that could affect the choices and behaviors of many supporters. Uninformed leaders whose behaviors don't align with expressed values and goals can cause reputational expenses, and they might lose their validity and the capacity to influence.

The fundamental first stage for leaders who wish to self-screen is to develop more prominent consciousness of our strengths and weaknesses as well as other strong internal factors including personal tendencies, needs, anxieties, predispositions, obstacles, and other bad behaviors. However, it isn't sufficient to just be self-aware. When it matters most, we should consider that knowledge, putting our brains in a position to alter our communication and behavioral patterns when our inner drives take over.

Regardless of where you end up in the progressive universe of work, whether your organizational structure is hierarchical, strongly matrixed, or Zappos-style, the capacity to understand yourself and communicate with others, the drive to find solutions to huge business challenges by managing throughout, and an emphasis on getting results by helping others succeed are resolute resources that will work well for you at each stage of your career.

CHAPTER 9

Acknowledging the Power of Gratitude

Gratitude is a positive emotion that includes being thankful and grateful and is related to a few mental and physical health benefits. When you experience gratitude, you feel appreciation for a person or thing in your life with sensations of graciousness, warmth, and different types of generosity.

The word *gratitude* can have various implications depending on how others use it and in what setting.

> *If we acquire a good through exchange, effort, or achievement, or by right, then we don't typically feel gratitude. Gratitude is an emotion we feel in response to receiving something good which is undeserved.*

—Michael Lacewing

History of Gratitude

This subject has intrigued strict researchers and rationalists since ancient times. However, research on gratitude didn't take off until the 1950s, as clinicians and sociologists investigated the effect that gratitude can have on people and groups. From that point forward, interest in the subject has developed extensively as the potential health benefits have become progressively more apparent.

Signs of Gratitude

So, what does gratitude look like? How can you say whether you are experiencing a feeling of gratitude? Communicating your appreciation and gratitude for what you have can occur in various ways. For instance, it could involve the following:

- Putting in time pondering the things in your life that you are appreciative for
- Stopping to notice and recognize the excellence or marvel of something you experience in your day-to-day routine
- Being thankful for your health
- Saying thanks to somebody for the positive impact they have on your life
- Doing something kind for someone else to show that you are thankful
- Focusing on the little things in your life that give you pleasure and harmony
- Reflection or prayer to God focusing on expressing gratefulness

We can classify gratitude in three unique ways:

1. As full of feeling, implying that it is connected with an individual's overall demeanor. Some individuals typically experience gratitude more often than others.

In spite of that, research has not shown an unmistakable association with any of the Big Five character qualities like principles, sociability, and extroversion.

2. As a mood that implies it might vary over time. Individuals might go through periods when they feel more appreciative as a rule, and at different times they might encounter this feeling on rare occasions.

3. As an emotion, which is a briefer feeling that individuals experience. Individuals could have specific experiences that produce feelings of gratitude.

Stages of gratitude:

1. First comes the affirmation of goodness in one's life. In a condition of gratitude, we say yes to life. We attest that life is excellent, all things considered, has things that make life worth living, and is abundant. The affirmation that we have gotten something satisfies us, both by its presence and the provider's work in picking it.

2. Second is perceiving that a portion of the wellspring of this goodness lies outside the self. One can appreciate others, animals, and the world, but not oneself. At this stage, we perceive the goodness in our lives and whom to thank for it, that is, who made sacrifices for our happiness.

The two stages of gratitude are acknowledging the goodness in our lives and the way this goodness came to us from outside ourselves. Then, finally, we perceive the karma of all that makes up our lives—and ourselves—better with this cycle.

Why is gratitude important? Consistently rehearsing and offering thanks has many advantages, both short-and long-term. Gratitude is a phenomenal way to mental prosperity.

Clinicians who have investigated gratitude view it as the fundamental focal point of positive brain science. There is some evidence that individuals who deliberately remember their good fortune are generally more joyful and less discouraged. How does this work?

- Gratitude changes our brains. Research has shown that individuals who tend to be more thankful have more brain activity in the prefrontal cortex, the region related to learning and direction. Furthermore, this brain activity endured a month later, suggesting that gratitude creates lasting impact.
- Gratitude can overwhelm negative emotions. Feeling appreciative lifts positive emotions like joy and sympathy while empowering us to search for and associate with what's great in life. This assists us with changing our point of view from toxic emotions, like hatred and jealousy.
- Gratitude works in the long term. Therefore, a continued gratitude practice starts having long-lasting effects on mood and behavior, which can increase over time.
- Gratitude can assist with combatting depression. One study showed that solitary, intense gratitude prompts a quick 10 percent increase in satisfaction and a 35 percent decrease in negative side-effects. When it turns into a habit, it can assist with forestalling anxiety and depression.

Gratitude has a dual meaning: a worldly one and a transcendent one. In its worldly sense, gratitude is a feeling that occurs in interpersonal exchanges when one person acknowledges receiving a valuable benefit from another. Gratitude is a cognitive-affective state that is typically associated with the perception that one has received a personal benefit that was not intentionally sought after, deserved, or earned but rather because of the good intentions of another person.

—Robert Emmons & Robin Stern

Gratitude supports our idealism.

As indicated in research by Drs. Robert A. Emmons and Michael E. McCullough, individuals who wrote a couple of sentences every week zeroing in on gratitude felt more hopeful.

It works on our health.

Besides decreasing and countering negative emotions, practicing gratitude is connected to other healthy ways of behaving, such as working out. Research has likewise connected gratitude with increased bone strength, less pain, a slower pulse, and a deeper, regenerating rest.

It prompts more grounded relationships and networks.

Through gratitude, we increase our ability to forgive, become likely to help, and foster sympathy for other people. In addition, gratitude can cause colleagues to feel more fulfilled and satisfied, conceivably diminishing the probability of burnout.

Scientists at the Wharton School at the University of Pennsylvania observed that laborers were 50 percent more productive when they had administrators who effectively gave thanks.

Close examination by clinicians Adam Grant and Francesca Gino found that getting gratitude for good work caused colleagues to feel major areas of strength in self-worth and certainty. It additionally prompted an expansion in trust and drove them to help one another.

It can prompt positive activities.

Whether communicating thankfulness or supporting other people, a respectful demeanor has been shown to improve our probability of spreading the consolation and joy it produces in us. Research proposes that gratitude may likewise take part in inspiring people to participate in positive ways of behaving, prompting self-improvement.

This can positively influence us on two levels. First, when we have a thankful mentality, we generally include ourselves in different practices that further develop our prosperity, like reflection, sports, and perceiving our assets. Second, it moves us to be kinder, smarter, and more selfless.

Likewise, research done by Frederickson showed that gratitude, when communicated, builds the likelihood of the beneficiary to loan favor to an outsider, successfully extending a network of good.

There are endless ways of showing our gratitude to other people, ourselves, and a higher power or even the universe itself. Be that as it may, it may be hard to get everything rolling without functional thoughts. These gratitude activities and exercises are the most notable and best-demonstrated ways of practicing and elevating your gratitude.

Journaling

Recording a few things you are thankful for is one of the simplest activities that anyone could hope to find.

The motivation behind the activity is to consider the previous day, days, or week, and recollect three to five things you are particularly appreciative of. Along these lines, you focus on every one of the beneficial things that happened to you in each time period.

What is the suitable measure of journaling one ought to do each week? Certain individuals propose doing it daily, while others recommend once a week. The contentions against doing it daily tend to be that it's boring and restrained. It turns into training you believe you ought to do or have to do instead of something you're happy to do.

When journaling turns into a chore and not an enjoyable practice, then you want to change how much journaling you do.

Other than the advantage of focusing on the brilliant things, this training can improve the nature of your rest, lessen the side effects of disease, and increase joy.

It is important to structure your training to what you want. Maybe journaling consistently for a short amount of time works for you, and later you discover it feels good to journal every Friday. Focusing on what you are thankful for becomes more straightforward as you practice it.

Envision your life without the things or individuals that make a difference to you before you start composing. That ought to help your gratitude indicator.

Gratitude Jar

The gratitude jar is an incredibly basic activity that can significantly affect your prosperity and viewpoint. It requires a few materials: a jar or box; a ribbon, stickers, glitter, or whatever else you like to embellish the jar; paper and a pen or pencil for composing your gratitude notes; and gratitude!

Step 1: Find a jar or box.

Step 2: Decorate the jar any way you wish. You can tie a ribbon around the jar's neck, put stickers on the sides, use clear paste and glitter to make it shimmer, paint it, keep it simple, or do whatever else you can imagine to make it pleasant to look at.

Step 3: This is the main step, which will be repeated consistently. Consider something like three things over the course of your day you are appreciative of. It may be something as small as an espresso at your favorite place or as major as the love for your soulmate or dear friend. Do this consistently. Record what you are thankful for on little pieces of paper and fill the jar.

Over the long haul, you will find that you have a jar brimming with many motivations to be thankful for what you have and enjoy the life you are living. It likewise will develop an act of communicating you will appreciate.

If you are feeling particularly down and need a quick jolt of energy, remove a couple of notes from the jar to help yourself remember who and what is great in your life.

Gratitude Rock

This exercise might sound somewhat senseless. "A rock? What can a rock do for me to practice gratitude?" The key to this exercise is that the rock is an image, an actual item you can use to help yourself remember what you have.

The directions are basic: simply track down a rock!

Make a point to pick one you like, whether you like it because it's pretty, smooth, or has an intriguing surface, or because you got it from a meaningful spot. If you have another little item you'd prefer to use, all things being equal, go ahead and substitute that for the rock.

Carry this rock around in your pocket or leave it in plain sight where you will see it over the course of your day, or even wear it on a chain around your neck or your wrist.

When you see it or touch it, think about something you are thankful for. Whether it's something as little as the sun shining down on you or as important as the job that permits you to take care of yourself or your family, simply think about one thing that gives you pleasure or satisfaction.

At the end of the day, when you take the stone from your pocket or off your body, pause for a minute and think about the things you were thankful for during the day. When you put it on or in your pocket again the next day, remember what you were thankful for yesterday and how it made you feel.

This will not only help you remember the things you are grateful for, but it can also give you a little boost to your day. It will free your thoughts for the current moment, offering you something for nothing in your consideration. It can likewise serve as a change to more positive thinking.

When you turn this switch on and off several times a day, you will probably find that your average day has become considerably more positive.

Gratitude Tree

The gratitude tree is an extraordinary experience for children. It can also be powerful for adults who are willing to experience a childlike sense of playfulness and wonder. You will require a few two-sided colored pieces of paper, string or ribbon, scissors, twigs or tree branches, a few stones or marbles, a container, and a feeling of gratitude.

Step 1: Make at least one leaf pattern to use as a layout for your leaves. Trace leaves on your shaded paper.

Step 2: Cut out the leaves. Poke a hole at the highest point of each leaf. Lace your string or ribbon through each opening.

Step 3: Put the stones or marbles in a jar and stick the tree limb or twig in the center.

Step 4: Have your child (or you yourself) draw or compose things that they or you are thankful for on the leaves. You can also use photos if you'd like.

Step 5: Hang the leaves from the branches and view your gratitude tree!

This project is simple and results in a lovely sign of the things that give you or your child pleasure throughout your daily routine. It could be planned for youngsters, yet there is no age limit on imaginative ways of developing your gratitude, so get to drawing!

Gratitude Garden

The gratitude garden activity is a great way to follow up on your gratitude trees. This is likewise planned for children; however, grown-ups can also get into this gratitude activity.

Follow these steps to journey to the gratitude garden.

1. Start the Journey: Stand up before your group with the Gratitude Tree in clear view. Announce that you are traveling to the Gratitude Garden, but to arrive,

you need to go through three hazardous spots. (Use a word other than *hazardous* if it is more suitable for the age group.) The Gratitude Tree will assist you with traversing each of these spots so you can make it to the Gratitude Garden.

2. The Frowny Forest: The first stop is the Frowny Forest. Have the children imitate you as you grimace, fold your arms, and slump over. There is a great deal of wind in the Frowny Forest. You're being thrown about by the breeze, turning around and back and forth as though you are attempting to battle it. The best way to leave the Frowny Forest is to feel cheerful once more, so ask the children to yell out things they are grateful for (using the Gratitude Tree as a source). After naming a couple of things, they display gratitude with a big grin.

3. The Sad Swamp: Goodness gracious! Just past the Frowny Forest is the Sad Swamp! Slouch over once more, swing your arms down low, and take big, heavy steps as though wading through mud or water. Once more, have the children yell out things they are grateful for so you can all leave the Sad Swamp.

4. The Mad Mountain: Past the Sad Swamp is the Mad Mountain. Have them copy you as you try to scale the mountain with extraordinary exertion, making crazy movements and faces. Once more, have the children yell out things they are grateful for so you can all feel blissful once more.

5. The Gratitude Garden: You have all arrived at the Gratitude Garden! What great work they have done! To celebrate, everybody can do a Happy Hop!

Gratitude Box

The gratitude box is a smart way to discuss your thoughts with friends and family and develop your own feelings of gratitude.

This simple activity requires a box, some paper, and a pen or pencil to record gratitude messages. You can make the box yourself or get one. The prettier, the better!

Write a simple message of gratitude to your loved one on the paper. If you don't know where to begin, here are a few ideas to start your message:

- "Thank you for…"
- "What I love about you…"
- "My vacation wish for you…"

You can likewise gather messages from others about your loved one to load the box with various messages of gratitude and love.

Place the message(s) in the box, wrap it up or put a bow on it, and give it to your loved one as an extraordinary gift to both them and yourself.

Gratitude Prompts

Gratitude prompts are a great method for beginners to continue with their training or start a slowed-down gratitude practice.

This is a generally straightforward activity with only one step: fill in the blank!

These prompts give multiple ways of starting a gratitude statement, with boundless opportunities for completion. They span a wide range of characteristics, species, people, and objects. The goal is to list three items for each sentence that you are thankful for.

- I'm grateful for three things I hear:
- I'm grateful for three things I see:
- I'm grateful for three things I smell:
- I'm grateful for three things I touch/feel:
- I'm grateful for three things I taste:
- I'm grateful for three blue things:
- I'm grateful for three animals:
- I'm grateful for three friends:
- I'm grateful for three educators:
- I'm grateful for three relatives:
- I'm grateful for three things in my home:
- I'm grateful for three individuals who employed me:

CHAPTER 10

Learning to Embrace Failure

What is failure? We all encounter it. Yet, certain individuals know how to learn from it to be more successful in the future. This chapter explores the significance of failure, the relationship between success and failure, and the reasons why people shouldn't be afraid of failing.

Attempting to avoid things on a consistent basis might end in failure, which can be painful and embarrassing. However, what is failure precisely?

Failure is characterized as a lack of success or the inability to fulfill an expectation. The problem is that we often internalize failure and set excessive unrealistic expectations for ourselves. Repeatedly, we attach it to our self-worth, confidence, and self-acknowledgment. The expectation we fail to meet is frequently our own or one we've made in our own mind.

The majority of us don't intend to fail at anything. Furthermore, we especially don't want to be perceived as a failure. However, perhaps that is a mistake. Failure can be useful, and we can learn from it, gain new bits of knowledge, and improve in the future. Certain failures provide us new information and insight that draws us nearer to our goals.

Some live by the witticism, "If you're not failing, you're not facing enough challenges." Said another way, if everything you do works out exactly as expected and feels great, you're most likely not extending yourself very far. What's more, on the off-chance you're not extending yourself, you're not developing.

Failure is defined as a nonappearance or absence of success. This is a universally useful definition, and it allows us to define success to know whether we have failed. The fundamental issue here is that most of us aren't perfect at characterizing success, and this can leave us feeling like failures. In reality, when the truth is told, we're the opposite. Working and living like this doesn't respect or regard the work we put into our lives. Now is the right time to redefine.

What definition of success and failure do you have right now? A few of us will not define either for ourselves. All things being equal, we'll let other individuals and the world around us define us. We'll be influenced by whoever impacts us most, whether that is our boss, closest companion, or celebrity we won't ever meet. This means that we're failing at whatever point we don't coordinate with their norms, and when we do, we're succeeding. Others might have an incomprehensibly narrow definition of success, which would make it hard to understand. If they live by this definition, they are more likely than not to fail. That is a hard lifestyle choice. And then there are those who never defines success and failure, meaning they don't have any idea what they are doing. That will cause everything to feel misguided or useless.

There is a compelling reason to classify everything as a success or a failure. However, there is no correct method for characterizing these states when called for. It's simply that a few definitions (or absence of) cause more damage than good. So, having said that, what definition could offer us the most advantage? Conceivably, basing the conditions of success and failure on values may make it most advantageous.

Failure is often seen as the absence or inability to achieve an objective. We often accept that determining whether you accomplished a goal is inherently clear-cut and easy. Be that as it may, in truth, failure is in many cases entirely subjective. Envision yourself in every one of these three situations and whether you'd see yourself as having failed:

- An experienced runner of a marathon puts forth a goal to run her next long-distance race in less than 4 hours and 30 minutes, which is 15 minutes less than her earlier best time. She finishes the long-distance race in 4 hours and 36 minutes, outclassing her earlier record by nine minutes.
- An aspiring employee looks for promotion to vice president and contends with other internal and external competitors. She gets positive criticism. Yet, she gets informed that the company felt that employing an outside individual would demonstrate their commitment to change.
- A top youthful expert at an association gets requested to set up a slide deck for a high-profile meeting. He submits

what he views as a phenomenal show to his boss. The manager praises the work yet substantially changes the slides before the huge meeting.

Notice that the differentiator in every one of the three of these examples is an ideal each person set for themselves. Estimating goal accomplishment can be an emotional and political movement. In every one of these examples above, you can detect that the people made a good attempt and performed well in their endeavors.

- It's possible that the standard definition of failure—not attaining a goal—isn't entirely accurate and clear.
- By what other method could we define failure?
- Reframing is a method used in training to rethink what is happening.

Photographers shift the lens around to get different angles of the same scene. We can likewise impact our point of view on circumstances to see them differently.

We can rethink failure using these equivalent terms:

Novice. When you're new at something, success is harder. For example, you can't set an assumption for a child to tie their shoes correctly the first time, or even the tenth. You can't compare yourself to the expertise of a master when you're a novice. When you attempt something new, adopt a novice's mentality. Remind yourself that you are a beginner and allow yourself numerous opportunities to get to the next level.

Learning an open door. Feeling dread about failure is probably the most common inhibitor of learning. One example is illustrated in the *Harvard Business Review* article "Teaching Smart People How to Learn."

Author Chris Argyris calls attention to the fact that numerous exceptionally successful individuals dread failure. They dread it explicitly because they have no expert involvement in it. As a result, they frequently respond defensively to failure. Additionally, they take actions to avoid it or make an effort not to notice it.

At the same time, they forgo the opportunity to learn and develop by trying something new and getting a different result than what was often predicted or expected. When something unexpected occurs, we have the opportunity to learn a lot about the situation and reevaluate our concerns. We have the opportunity to discover more about who we are and how we respond to misfortunes and the unexpected.

Perfectionism. Assuming you have areas you excel in, you might mark things as failures that are not. For instance, you could make a mistake when performing in a meeting with top executives. Despite incredible feedback from everyone involved, you concentrate on the one second that didn't go exactly as you had planned.

When whipping yourself for a past failure, ask yourself, "Have I failed? Or was I merely not perfect?"

Systemic bias. Such biases are practices or beliefs that are built into a system that hinder various groups. In the contemporary working world, systemic bias continues against ethnic minorities. They likewise endure against women, individuals with handicaps, and the LGBTQ+ community. For the vast majority of them, it tends to be the underlying driver of their apparent failure.

Surya Bonaly was one of only a handful of exceptional Black skaters during the 1990s. She got judged more critically for not typifying the "white princess" ideal in women's figure skating. People passed judgment on her and said she was "interesting" and "athletic but not creative."

The degree to which systemic bias impacted her Olympics failures can never be completely known. Have you thought about the systemic bias in your organization, which could be a reason why it fails?

Uncertainty. Our universe is progressively equivocal and inconsistent. Who would have thought that a global pandemic could start in 2019, and that it would turn the world of work on its head?

In some situations, it's almost impossible to avoid failure, especially when things are very unstable, unclear, complicated, or uncertain. So cut yourself and your partners a little leeway if a deadline is missed or if you've discovered a few errors in a project.

There might be different elements causing interruption and stress. When there is a decreased likelihood of achieving a goal due to uncertainty, either adjust the objective or course of action.

Try to spot mistakes brought on by confusion or a lack of common sense, but be aware of how often the best-laid plans may be derailed by unforeseen circumstances. Instead of lamenting the fact that circumstances changed your preferred ideas, concentrate on what your group can learn about working better under the reality of stress, interruption, and unpredictability.

Trial and error. A key tenet of the tech industry is to fail fast and learn from it. This mentality embraces failure as a characteristic piece of innovative strategy. Trial and error provides the chance to improve things consistently.

As Thomas Edison said about how many attempts it took to invent the lightbulb, "I haven't failed; I've just found ten thousand ways that won't work." When you see your failures as ways to improve, you have created another tool for success.

Restored inspiration. Sometimes a little setback turns into a hardship that sparks a renewed commitment to a project or goal. You might have subliminally placed the goal on autopilot or become occupied by different needs.

Failure may serve as a catalyst for boosting motivation and inspiration where it would otherwise have lagged. As poet Amanda Gorman famously put it, "Not broken but simply incomplete." Something that looks failed or broken may just be a distortion of an incomplete cycle.

Learn to Embrace Failure

We all realize failure isn't the apocalypse. However, that perception is difficult to embrace. Anxiety about failure, and failure itself, can subvert our leadership styles, execution,

Learning to Embrace Failure

judgment, and surprisingly, our joy. This week, embrace your fear of failure and get confidence from it in the following three ways:

1. Use fear to focus; however, don't allow it to dominate your attention.

Fear is a strong sensation; it may be an extraordinary resource or keep you down. Use it as a template since it indicates where you should truly focus your attention, the last elements that need to be wrapped up, and any flaws in your plan or product. When you see the indication, focus on it directly and let the uncomfortable feeling go. Try using fear this week as a source of insight by observing it from a distance. Then, note the indicator and how you plan to respond to whatever provoked it. Does giving the indicator some serious thought help you get some relief, clear your head, and get moving forward?

2. Allow your group to fail to build its success.

Groups that dread failure and its outcome convey unremarkable outcomes over the long haul. This occurs as a result of the fact that they labor and are paid for predictable results, rather than those that are more probable. How will you respond when they miss the mark? Make use of common language and interactions to describe determined outcomes and stretch goals week after week in order to motivate your team to realize previous expectations. Your team will be motivated to go above and beyond expectations if you use a procedure that acknowledges and commends both the achievement of predetermined goals as well as the effort made when the goal isn't realized.

125

3. Consider your failures as starting points as opposed to endings.

Failure is as inescapable as death and taxes and can make us feel extremely uncomfortable! Yet, every failure opens new opportunities and presents new insight. Rather than dwelling on the failure, concentrate on the knowledge gained and the new opportunities presented. Think about five past failures. What did you learn? Might you not be where you are currently without these lessons? You've likely learned more from failure than any other source of knowledge. As opposed to feeling fear and inconvenience, embrace failure's ability to teach, become interested in the information it offers, and be open to where it leads you next. (You might try and find you fail less when you don't fear it.)

Long-term, you can shift your focus to feel successful from processes and outcomes. The construction set forth by Atomic Habits creator James Clear may be useful to you, where he recognizes three phases of failure:

Failure of vision is when you are not satisfied with what you need or your own "why," when you don't have the foggiest idea of what you deeply desire. In addition, you can be experiencing a failure of vision if you don't feel that your life has meaning and worth.

This is where searching internally and focusing on your happiness can affect you.

Failure of strategies is when you know what you need but don't have a valid or clear plan for accomplishing it. For example, perhaps you've failed to finish a project, since you just have a general idea and not a groundbreaking strategy.

Indeed, even people who are great at preparation in the work environment occasionally struggle, particularly when translating such skills into tactics for developing one's leadership abilities. This is where monitoring propensity and improvement can be exceptionally viable.

Failure of the system is when you have a process and follow it, yet don't accomplish your goal. An endless number of variables could be influencing your success, and they might be connected or irrelevant to your process.

Technical failure is the best opportunity to use your strategic thinking skills and begin working on the next cycle.

Understanding why you feel failure can assist you with defeating difficulties in your interaction results. Perhaps reflecting on this will result in "recharged motivation" to carry out your objectives. Remember that not a single one of us can avoid failure constantly. That isn't the aim.

The reality is that our success as people and groups relies upon us learning in order to perform better. If we aren't failing regularly, we likely aren't facing an adequate number of challenges.

Again and again, we mentally embrace trial and error and risk. We maintain that we should do it effectively and neatly without failing, but that shouldn't be the goal.

The goal should be to be strong in spite of failure. A tough individual will adopt these qualities in the process of goal fulfillment:

- Self-empathy. Offer grace to yourself as well as other people engaged with the failure. Focus on compassion and keeping the failure in context. There's a contrast between conceding failure and punishing yourself for it.

- Mental peace. Be able to learn from failures and turn to new open doors rapidly.

- Growth attitude. Adopt a learner's strategy with a non-critical position. As a matter of course, we answer defensively or cast blame. Reflect profoundly and attempt to comprehend how to go ahead.

- Critical thinking. Remain curious and innovative. Gather information to illuminate choices and following stages.

- Reason and significance. Try not to complain. Reconnect with the greater importance behind the goal and use that to drive new methodologies.

- Acknowledgment. Value the effort that you and others have made up to this point. Feel successful by gauging the interaction as much as or more than the result.

CHAPTER 11

Continuing to Evolve

In a world consumed by image, one winds up lost among an ocean of fakes. You see individuals around you showing how successful they are, how blissful they are, how accomplished they are, while you may be stuck and burdened by serious insecurity. Society is so worried about image that anything short of what we collectively consider a success is viewed as a disappointment. Did you find a new line of work? Big deal—anybody can get a job. Have you earned a college diploma? So what—anybody can do that. Did you travel abroad? Congrats—so did ten million other Instagram members last year. As a result, you try to do more and demonstrate that you achieved something truly substantial. Nothing remains to be finished. However, you are still the same person who was previously browsing other people's accounts for virtual enjoyment. You haven't evolved; you haven't changed; as a matter of fact, you could be stuck because what you have been endeavoring to do is how society has advised you to be successful.

Evolving as an individual means growing personally rather than just going through the motions of life. You don't need to worry about the thing others are doing. You need to understand that what you consider success awards you harmony, not what others accept is a success. When that's what you understand, you will find that you can carry on with your desired existence. Life isn't intended to be broadcast; it is intended to be recollected, because the recollections you love the most are, in many cases, the ones that lack external confirmation that they actually occurred.

Evolving as a person originates from understanding being human, living in the moment, interfacing with others, and arriving at a specific equilibrium. Your morality, beliefs, and actions characterize you. The best method to evaluate anything is to have a reflective grasp of it. Your way of evolving is by learning from past experiences, which is how you can relate to others on a human level.

This can be quite challenging in a company, because business is just about bringing in cash and establishing commercial relationships. This challenge originates from separating emotion from responsibility and simultaneously neglecting to focus on yourself personally. A detailed understanding of yourself can transform these challenges into opportunities to improve personally. Motivate yourself to learn more, comprehend more, interact more, and genuinely improve.

You may not believe that you can consciously direct your own growth. However, there is mounting evidence that all of us can develop our conscious selves, which controls our personality, mental capabilities, emotions, and behavior. We normally think of development as real changes across time, but recent perspectives suggest that some development occurring right now may be prompted by a need or want.

For instance, the well-known wildlife writer and photographer Boyd Norton captured on film a monkey that suddenly began to walk and run upright. And the Moken people of Southeast Asia, who depend on the ocean for their way of life, were able to develop the capacity for underwater vision by exerting a significant amount of force on the pupil. While these are not the sorts of thing everyone can do, it demonstrates how need or desire provokes change.

"Those who do not move do not notice their chains."

This serves as a conclusive summation for this chapter, since as you grow and change other people no longer depend on you; not because they don't care about you, but rather because they may project their sense of restraint onto you. Those who stay put won't realize they are constrained by a way of living that prevents them from bettering their surroundings or themselves. As you work on yourself, you will grow out of your current circumstance and even some of the people in your life. Unfortunately, this is only a reality since there are individuals who won't move and refuse to see the chains.

Whether those are chains of refusal, dread, or something different, some attempt to improve, and some don't venture out because they "know" nothing will come of it.

This segment is about you improving yourself and what happens when everyone around you maintains that you should remain where you are. Assuming you break free from your chains, it might imply that they'll need to break free from theirs as well.

Furthermore, it sounds uncomfortable. So uncomfortable that those who don't step out will never understand how a small period of awkwardness may lead to a lifetime of healing and fulfillment. Those initial steps are the hardest to take; specific individuals don't believe you should take them. They aren't prepared to evolve, so they don't need you to buy into the same token.

Practice appreciation. Check the great parts out. One of my clients broke his neck in a fender-bender and suffered other serious wounds. He offered thanks for his life in many meetings and investigated how he needed to make the most out of each day. He recuperated more rapidly than anticipated and today is without stress. We acknowledge and value this discussion about the strength of the brain-body connection. Appreciation brings more goodness and optimism into life.

Give up defensiveness. Save yourself and every one time by eliminating excuses. Be mindful of projection, rationalization, denial, and rejection, and take a sincere look in the mirror. Seek therapy, support, or a twelve-step group, as well as the insight of old buddies and family. When we let down our protective shield, we can take care of our more profound responsibilities and develop.

Practice acceptance. Try not to be dismissive or fall victim to traps. Avoid wasting energy fighting or resisting what you cannot change (others, their sentiments, their ways of behaving, and so forth). Instead, empower yourself to change what you can (your reasoning, ways of behaving, limits, and so on).

Excuse and let go of feelings of depression. Allow yourself to forgive and free yourself from negative encounters of the past. In times of prayer or reflection, be thankful for the knowledge and understanding that came through your suffering. Practice the mantra, "I excuse you, and I release you."

Be authentic. Be real and genuine. Have the mental fortitude and certainty to act naturally. Try to avoid making bogus statements, even to yourself.

Reflect empathy. Relinquish the requirement for judgment. Instead, imagine another person's perspective, consider how they feel, and reflect that to them appropriately.

Be immediate. Say what you mean and mean what you say. The truth will release you. Chat with the people you know, even if you aren't fond of them, instead of seeking others. Stay away from blunt or aggressive strategies in an attempt to make a point (not answering messages or calls, and so on).

Be caring and humane. Participate in conversation with others, assuming they are thoughtful, essential, and valid. Help other people. Think about the wants and needs of others before any activity.

Be honest. Do what you say you will do. If things have changed and you are moving another way, tell the truth and be transparent with others. Be solid and predictable. Concede when you are off-base. If appropriate, you should apologize and offer to remedy the situation.

Love yourself. Practice self-sympathy and taking care of oneself. Understand you are precisely as you ought to be and are completely adorable as you are. Forgive yourself and understand you are human, and no one is perfect. Commend your life, your exceptional soul, and your gifts. Take significant consideration of yourself and surround yourself with individuals who love you, want the absolute best for you, and will assist as you grow.

What Evolution Looks Like

Changing Doesn't Work

First, let's explain the distinction between changing and evolving. To change suggests turning into an alternate individual or modifying an essential identifying characteristic. For instance, this could involve attempting to change somebody from introverted to extroverted. An introverted individual likes to work alone, re-energizes by doing activities freely, and succeeds from alone time. To change them into an extrovert by compelling them to work in a consistent joint effort with individuals or constantly associate with individuals without breaks would push them to neutralize their natural assets. It would simply not work and also make the individual extremely despondent. They could possibly support the change for a brief time; however, they would return to their regular style at some point.

Evolving Does Work

To evolve is to make improvements to things that already work for you so you can focus on enhancing your results. In the case of the introvert, they might find their withdrawn nature is sometimes ruining their success since they struggle with working in a group or speaking out at gatherings, and/or social settings.

They need to develop into the kind of person who can simulate extroverted behavior when it's necessary. As far as they might be concerned, venturing into their power could impart their insight and lives to individuals to make different connections and further develop equality. This slight change (development) considers growth without undermining their regular inclinations. The benefit is that the loner will probably find they appreciate being around individuals, being heard, and sharing thoughts for however long is needed, as long as it's not excessive and they get breaks. A person faking being an extrovert when required drives themselves to improve as a variant of themselves. They will flourish with exemplary meaningful activities yet want to conform to extroverted behavior to drive improved results.

Evolving Allows Us to Fail

Perceiving that we are continually working to evolve ourselves is a significant piece of the journey and is fundamental to success. Recognizing this empowers us to consider growth through experimentation. This gives us the necessary courage to fail. When we make it about change, there is an inordinate amount of contrast between the two. We are set up to fail in a mindset of change because constantly changing is unthinkable. We can succeed with a mindset of evolving because it's working slowly off our assets, leading not exclusively to greater wins yet to a seriously fulfilling life.

Evolving Is Meant to Be Selfish

The objective isn't to evolve for the good of any other person; this is a selfish undertaking. So we venture into our power for ourselves. We make better versions of ourselves for our own happiness and success. And from that difficult work, we find that everybody develops around us.

Evolution of Relationships

Stage 1: In their most simplistic form, relationships based on love are driven by the basic needs for survival: food, shelter, and sex. Our fundamental sexual decision process is determined from this level and experienced when we drop any reasonable or moral objections to become sexual with another individual.

Stage 2: At a higher level, there is the development of a deep spiritual connection with one's partner. This emotion is associated with higher states of consciousness. This is often depicted in fantasies, over-romanticized movies, and romance novels. We experience this type of love when we sense that we can't survive without a particular individual who causes us to feel (psychologically) complete. A few specialists refer to this as "commonly possible pathologies."

Stage 3: Following this spiritual stage, we want a partner who makes us happy by giving us what we've always needed and what we deserve now, someone who generously takes care of all our needs and wants while giving up their own. If the person fails to do what we want, we demand to be loved, supported, recognized and respected, and we are quick to reject our partner and end the friendship.

Stage 4: As we evolve further, we come to realize that sexuality and spirituality are intertwined. Heartfelt sentiments don't equal love, yet "genuine love" isn't an inclination but rather an interaction that is represented by principles like permanent responsibility, humility, kindness, contrition, commitment, and "marriage 'til death do us part." Isolating oneself from a partner is unacceptable. If we do so, we open ourselves up to a huge personal responsibility, and the possibility of being judged by someone in a more powerful position of authority.

Stage 5: In the following phase of love, we understand that successful couples support each other in understanding their most significant potential for self-realization, professional and individual success, opportunity, sexual satisfaction, ideal emotional and physical well-being, abundance, and joy.

Stage 6: When we've done everything we can to achieve success together and find happiness through a partner, spiritual love without limits or "true love" is possible. We see an inward abundance of a higher love that likewise streams out to every conscious being. As the Medieval poet Rumi stated, "Our errand isn't to seek for love, simply to seek and track down every one of the boundaries inside ourselves that we have worked against." Many types of love relationships grow out of this level, and we can love numerous individuals who love us and all others consequently (with the performative inconsistency that we alienate individuals who we see as un-cherishing—to be specific, individuals in stages 4, 5, and 7).

Stage 7: We escape the "everything goes" varieties of love in the previous stage when we coordinate the sound viewpoints and insights of past relationships and rise above their restricted perspectives. This lets us work together to make a serious relationship in which we meet each other's physical, sexual, emotional, intellectual, social, and mental needs. We do this by agreeing to love, resolve, learn, and grow together.

Stage 8: The most recent development of love relationships is between couples who completely exemplify the past "indispensable" level and offer a genuine transformative reason. They are committed to helping each other in their quest for more profound mental healing and higher spiritual recognition. At the same time, as a couple with similar limits, they are ready to help move humanity toward a peaceful and fair future that will last forever. By moving forward together into the unknown, these couples do the most good for the most people through their true transformative purpose.

There will be disharmony in a relationship between two people at different stages of their development, who are neurotically attached to the limits of previous stages, or who haven't fully risen above and included the good ideas or important limits of each previous stage. At times, groundbreaking integral training or integral therapy can give an answer; in other cases, cutting off the friendship with love and empathy serves the two partners best.

Conclusion

If you look around you, there is always a creature that can inspire you, be it people, birds, animals, insects, plants, or Mother Nature. However, it depends on your point of view.

There have been many historical accounts in which people are inspired by a tiny insect like an ant. Once, an army commander deserted his troops and hid in a cave to avoid being humiliated. One day, he saw an ant carrying food a bit bigger than itself. Every time it climbed the wall, it fell back, but it tried again until it finally reached its destination.

The commander thought about the power he had compared to the tiny creature. He got up and vowed to face the enemy with all the strength he had. He led his battalion and won the battle.

Therefore, whenever you feel down or think negatively, there is so much around you from which to take an inspirational lesson. It could come to you in any shape and size. All you need is the intent to learn and grow.

Takeaways

- Meeting with yourself entails getting to know yourself at a much deeper level.
- Living and growing are parallel; when you stop living, you stop growing, and vice versa.
- A few bad experiences in life do not make you a bad person.
- Take every challenge as another golden opportunity to learn and grow.
- Learn to respect yourself before expecting others to respect you.
- A disability is not an obstacle to success. The only obstacles are in your mind.
- A burning desire breaks through the biggest of obstacles.
- Success speaks louder than excuses.
- If you are stuck in life, analyze your thoughts.
- A "should" from our loved ones can frequently sabotage us.
- You realize your true potential when you persist despite obstacles.
- Your age doesn't stop you from growing, but your attitude can.